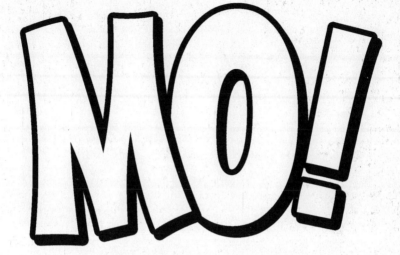

MO!

Everyday Heroes
Who Live With
MOmentum,
MOtivation
and
MOxie

Shawn Doyle & Lauren Anderson

sound wisdom
Shippensburg, PA

Sound Wisdom

167 Walnut Bottom Road, Shippensburg, PA 17257-0310

To find out about ordering this book, call 386-227-7814.

Reach us on the Internet: www.soundwisdom.com

ISBN13 TP: 978-1-937879-03-7

Ebook 13 ISBN: 978-1-937879-07-5

For Worldwide Distribution, Printed in the U.S.A.

3 4 5 6 7 8 / 16 15

Contents

Introduction

Hello! Welcome to MO! I am Shawn Doyle and this is Lauren Anderson. Thanks for joining us. We are both professional speakers, trainers, and consultants. We have been doing what we do for over sixty years combined and we have learned some valuable lessons. We have both met, trained, coached, developed, and mentored thousands and thousands of people in different parts of the world throughout our careers both as corporate employees and as entrepreneurs who own our own respective companies. Over those years, we noticed something independently and then together, and that is how the story of MO! begins.

How MO! Was Born

It all started in a delivery room in Tampa, Florida, when the OB/GYN announced, "Congratulations you have a baby MO!" No, not really, we're just kidding. It started in a pub in England when someone said, "Kill 'em MO!" No, that's not right either. It actually started as a conversation Lauren and I were having one day. She was telling me about this amazing man who was a service advisor at an automobile dealership. As she excitedly told me his story, I was blown away! I said, "So let me get this straight: customers actually *call* to see if he is there at the dealership—and if he isn't, they wait to bring their car in to be serviced?" She said yes. Then she told me they actually come to the dealership and take him out to lunch! As my British friends would say, I was "gobsmacked!" How could this be? I then said to her, "That reminds me of a taxi driver I met in Washington, DC, who wore a suit, tie, and hat and whose taxi was so immaculate you could eat off the floor." She said, "You mean a limousine?" I said, "No, a taxi." I also then told her that he was the official taxi for many congressmen and senators who preferred him to a limo and also, by the way, paid him limo rates. Lauren could not believe it. So as we continued to bring up our various stories and examples we came to a realization. It was like a bolt of lightning, a defining moment. These people had something! They all had a certain "Je ne sais quoi"—an indescribable, beautiful, magical quality about each of them. What *was it?* These were people in ordinary jobs, or maybe different jobs that weren't ordinary—but despite life experiences and adversity, they decided *not* to be ordinary. They performed their jobs brilliantly, exceptionally, differently and exceeded everyone's expectations of what that job "should" be every day. More important, everyone around them knew it, saw it, and acknowledged it. We see it in the special people that we meet as we travel and in the people we meet in the classroom and after keynote speeches. They stand out. They shine. So it was driving us crazy—what was *this quality?* We finally figured it out, nailed it down, and gave it a name: MO!

So What Is MO!?

Are you thinking maybe it's one of the three stooges? No, that was Moe (with Larry and Curly and Shemp).

Mo can stand for many things, but MO! stands for the following:

- *MOmentum.* These people are a force that creates the energy to make things go forward, but more than that, they are momentum.

- *MOtivated.* These people are massively self-motivated, and they even motivate others around them through the power of their special spark. It is contagious.

- *MOst extraordinary.* You would never accuse these people of ever being ordinary, despite the fact they hold what some people could say are ordinary or even mundane jobs. However, these jobs are not mundane to them.

- *MOxie.* They have the courage, the ambition, and the initiative to take their jobs and turn them into something different. No one told them to; they just did!

- *MOnumental.* Their qualities are so special they become monuments or landmarks and an attraction unto themselves, sometimes even over and above their business itself.

- *MOtion.* They are always moving, innovating, and finding new ways to create in their jobs. They are never satisfied with the same old way. Ever.

- *MOre.* They do MO!, get MO!, make MO!, and sell MO!

- *MOjo.* They have some magical, mystical quality that makes them charm almost every person they meet. They could charm the rattles off a snake.

So here is our official definition of MO!

MO! (noun or adjective)—*1. people in ordinary jobs who perform at extraordinary levels with MOtivation, MOmentum, and MOxie. 2. a special, unique quality that makes people stand out and become a force of excitement and energy. 3. a difference maker. 4. people who are not in ordinary jobs but still have " it"(you know it when you see it)* (e.g., Boy, that Victor, he sure has some kind of MO!).

Why You Need MO!

Simply put, this modest little book could transform your life if you let it. Why? Because once you have MO! and apply it, you will have MO! of everything in your life: MO! money, MO! sales, MO! love, MO! friends, MO! satisfaction, MO! joy, MO! hair.

OK, we were kidding on the hair part. (Our attorney made us say that.) But seriously, people are magnetically attracted to people with MO! like moths to an energy-saving yellow light bulb. Aren't you? Aren't you attracted to people with passion and energy? Don't deny it—the MO! chip in this book has a GPS, and we will track you down! You know it is the truth. We are willing to help you get it. You know you want it, you need it, you have it inside of you somewhere. We are going to help you bring out *your* MO!

How Do You Get MO!?

You may have MO! or someone you know may have it. We assume that if you already have it, you want more of it. (Don't you?) If you don't have it, you want it. How do you get it? Well, as the world's only MO!tivational speakers (for now), we know the MO! secrets and we are willing to share. We interviewed each of the special people in this book who have MO! and we were inspired by them. We have been able to determine the special four to six qualities each of these special people have—and we have been able to boil down the essence of each of our subjects. Here is the exciting part: we are going to provide the secrets to their very special qualities and give you tips and techniques on how you can learn them.

Can it be learned? Yes, we think so. Sure, some people are just naturals and have a high level of MO! already. But we think they are the exceptions, not the rule. Many of us didn't start out with MO!; we had people who inspired and taught us along the way in life and then one day, BLAM! We had MO! We believe if you teach someone the attributes of people who have MO! and then let them work on it, combined with the right environment, we will have something special and they will have MO! Think about it: we are the only species (as far as we know) who have the ability to change our lives through conscious thought, should we decide to. We don't think you would be reading this book if you weren't ready. So are you really, totally ready?

How This Book Works

I was teaching a class at a bank in Charlotte, North Carolina. I was talking about motivation and passion. I wanted to make a point about passion and I needed to describe passion. In a spontaneous, improvisational moment, I said, "Passion is like...well, like Chiliman!" The class roared. All twenty-five people knew Chiliman by name! Chiliman, by the way, is Victor Wernay, the guy who serves hot dogs outside of the building one day a week (only on Thursdays). I had watched him in action the week before. Huh? Why would they remember him? He doesn't even work for the bank. Why? He has MO!

In this book you will read inspiring profiles of a service advisor, hot dog vendor, airline gate agent, seafood market owner, construction worker, fitness trainer, taxi driver, professional speaker, and an entrepreneur who all have the magic MO! qualities. They are all normal people who work every day, but their work isn't normal.

At the end of each profile you will see a summation of the four to six special qualities that they have and our suggestions on how to incorporate them into your life and how *you* can get more MO!

We see people who are getting tired of media stars who are rich, are privileged, were born with silver spoons in their mouths, and may even be famous for being famous or just stupidly lucky. We want to make our subjects the stars of MO! They worked hard and made their own luck. As you will see, they were never handed anything except an opportunity and sometimes a paycheck. We believe they are the real heroes and because they have done it, it might be easier to believe that you can do it, and you can.

Our goal is to make a difference in the world, and we think by sharing these MO! stories you can make a difference too.

One quick note about how to use this book; you will see at the end of each chapter two segments: one is *MO! Notes,* and the other is *meMO.* Each of these segments has a very specific purpose. *MO! Notes* are designed to summarize some of the key learning points from that particular person's life. Next you will see the section called *meMO.* Back in the old days in offices, there used to be an item called a memo. (Some of you may be old enough to remember this.) The word *memo* is short for "memorandum." In essence, a memo is a piece of paper with important information. Our version is a memo to yourself or, as it is written, a *meMO!* (OK, we know that sounds a little caveman-like—"me mo!"—but at least it's memorable.) In these segments you will find several suggestions on how to specifically apply the learning points to your life. All these suggestions are observable, measurable, and tangible. That way they are not just vague ideas or concepts but techniques you can apply to your life *now*. Comprende my friende?

So let's get MO!ving with our first story.

1

Victor Wernay:
Chiliman

When we first saw "Chiliman" in Charlotte, North Carolina, we were amazed. Chiliman was outside of a bank building on a Thursday and had a long line of people who were patiently waiting to be served. While people were waiting in line, Chiliman kept up a constant patter of comedic lines and people were laughing and joking along with him. He would ask people if they would like "Fluffy Bunny" mustard or his world-famous custom Merlot-B-Que sauce (made with merlot wine) on their hot dogs, both his own brands. While standing in line, people could read various funny signs like "Chili dogs making you smarter-er," "If you lined up all the hot dogs we have ever served, it would really go a long way," and "I am the only son of an only son of an only son." When you think about it, this is extraordinary. Hot dog vendors are supposed to serve food; they're not supposed be a source of entertainment and a boost for morale. They are usually boring and not memorable. But that is not and never has been how Victor Wernay (a.k.a. Chiliman) does things. "It was never about hotdogs," he says. "It was always about becoming a legend." The way he says this is remarkable because it sounds like a passionate mission and not a statement of ego.

Victor started his career working in and around various restaurants and food service businesses. He worked in pizza places, coffee shops, and other casual dining venues. He once worked as a manager of a pizza parlor and realized that he most of all loved serving and interacting with people. At this pizza parlor he created a very unique approach. Each time children came in with their families, they got to color a picture and write their names on it, and then it was posted somewhere on the walls of the restaurant. Eventually the entire interior of the restaurant was covered with children's drawings and colored pictures. This led to an interesting phenomenon: children would bring their families in to show off their work. It meant a significant increase in business and it was a very popular and unique feature of the pizza parlor. Unfortunately, as Victor relates, upper management decided that it was "too much" and decided to take all the pictures down, which led to a significant dip in business.

At a coffee place where Victor worked, he loved joking around with customers and was always able to put smiles on their faces, but he soon grew weary of his manager's approach. The manager once criticized him for having coffee stains on the counter. Victor responded, "Well of course there's coffee stains on the counter, it's a coffee place!" The behaviors and mindset of the corporate world and their obsession with the bottom-line "over the interest of people" was driving Victor crazy.

Victor and his wife decided to take a vacation and travel around Europe for a while. They both had a lot of time to think. One day when they were driving around, Victor asked his wife, "What do you think I should do?" She paused briefly and then said, "I think you should own a hot dog cart," and smiled. Victor asked her if she was joking and she said, "No, I think you have all the skills and abilities to own a hot dog cart. You have background and experience in food service and the personality to make the thing successful." He thought about the idea for several weeks and asked friends about it, because for some reason it seemed like a silly idea to him. All his friends were very supportive and thought he should go for it. He researched the cost of buying a hot dog cart and the licensing required, and as he says, "Sometimes you have a combination of good timing and luck." As luck would have it, a hot dog vendor at a popular corner in downtown Charlotte happened to quit and that space became available two days a week. The rest, as they say, is history. The former comedian and actor set up a hot dog stand at the corner of Fourth and Tryon.

Victor says, "People have a choice when they get up every day. They can have a bad day or a good day. I choose to have a good day." He started talking up the crowds that lined up, and he had a new crazy saying on his sign every day. "I try to make a personal connection with each person. I think people really crave connection. It's a human need. I try to make a personal connection on some fact. It might be the weather, their name, the sports news of the day, whatever." He smiles and says, "Any boob with four thousand dollars can be a hot dog guy, but I want to *the* hot dog guy—Chiliman!"

"One other lesson I learned early," says Victor, "is if people are slightly happy, and not thinking about their wait in line, they don't mind as much. Secondly (I learned this in the restaurant business), the people in the back of the line need to be acknowledged, and as long as they are, they will stay too."

The business began to build, and without actually seeking locations, he landed two days a week outside bank offices and an additional day outside a law school. People were amused by his very unique sauce names. "I notice things," says Victor, "and I thought the sauce names you see in stores for barbeque and especially hot sauces are awful and scary. You know, names like 'Hot Sauce Suicide' or something like 'Skull Splitting Sauce' with an evil-looking skull on it. Who wants to eat that? So I have come up with names that sound better and more edible and nice, like 'Fluffy Bunny' (for mustard) and 'Fluffier Bunny' (for spicier mustard) and 'Cuddly Baby Bar-B-Que' (for mild sauce) and 'God's Gift to Bar-B-Que' (you have to taste it)." Why use such crazy product names? "I am not really totally sure why, but I have always had a kind of obsession with naming things. When I was acting I had a card that said, 'Victor Wernay: actor, comedian, and legendary model for the visually impaired.'" He chuckles. "I know it's not politically correct, but they still remember the card. My goal is simple: (1) to make people laugh and (2) to be remembered—not just for the product but also remembered as me." He has one hot sauce, one ketchup, five mustards, six mayonnaises, and five barbeque sauces. "I just love playing around with the food."

Victor's early years were shaped by a father who had a dry wit and a mother who was extremely extroverted. She acted in plays and would play the accordion for anyone who would listen, "and no one wanted to hear the accordion. No one ever does!" His Aunt Jeanetta was the "loose cannon" of the family; her loony humor at family get-togethers kept them all laughing and perhaps also shaped Victor's own brand of humor today. He was also influenced by a drama teacher in high school named Art Gage. Art taught Victor's drama class but more importantly encouraged him to get involved in Project Adventure, an Outward-Bound-style program. This built his confidence.

Victor thinks his keys to success look deceptively simple but are hard to learn. "Always go for the personal connection. I go into a Sam's Club store to buy supplies and everybody who works there knows me, is glad to see me, greets me. I gotta tell ya, it blows my friends' minds. I may take it to the extreme, but people love to be connected with—everyone."

Once, on a hot day, a man came up to his cart with a dog and ordered a hot dog, a soda, and a bottle of water. Victor handed him the hot dog, the soda, the bottle of water, and a cup. The man looked at the cup and said,

"What is the cup for?" Victor smiled and said, "The cup is for your dog. I know the soda is for you; the water is for your dog." The man was amazed, but as Victor says, "That is the extra touch, the extra mile. That is service, the little details." His service is so great that he averages about 15 percent in tips each day in addition to the regular revenue. No one tips hot dog guys, right?

Victor has customers that are so loyal that they walk by his cart and say in a guilty tone, "I'm sorry I can't buy your food today, I have to go to a business luncheon." The bond Victor creates makes them feel obligated!

Victor says, "The irony is I have never chased anything. I am doing what I do and it just happens. New locations get offered; people ask me to set up at festivals. It just happens that way." He is working on a possible deal to package and distribute his sauces. "They met me and asked me—like I said, it just happens."

As we leave Victor Wernay, Chiliman, he's wearing a crazy hat and joking with a woman about her name. She is laughing and smiling while she is buying a hot dog.

MO! Notes

1. **Connect.** Go out of your way to find some method or technique to connect with people. In an age of technology and impersonal communication, people want to be connected in a personal, individual way. As Victor says, "They crave it."

2. **Be original.** The signs with the funny sayings, the humor, and the original sauce names; they

are all original and, more important, memorable. We simply forget the average, but we
remember the extraordinary and unique. We
also tell our friends about the extraordinary
and unique, creating buzz and word-of-
mouth advertising (the best kind).

3. **Serve people.** When you serve people and
   don't worry about rules, regulations, and
   things being too much, people respond.
   Well-meaning managers eliminate things
   people like for their own business reasons,
   but they are not the reasons of the customers. The consequence is angry customers and
   lost business.

4. **Reinvent your category.** There were plenty
   of hot dog stands before Chiliman's, but
   by using unique approaches and ideas, he
   changed his category. He has no competition.
   People want to wait in line for the food and
   the show.

5. **Be observant.** Look around at the world, the
   business, and your customers. Think about
   what they want. Watch what they do. Look at
   products and try to make them better. Look
   at every detail. Look at the products' names
   and packaging and how they are sold. Keep
   your eyes open to opportunity.

meMO!

- Think about your business or your role at the
  business you work for. Make a list of things

that your customers respond to positively. Try to make changes that are in accordance with that list.

- Pull out a piece of paper. On that paper write down a list of at least five ways you can connect better with your customers. They might be ways to connect on social media such as Twitter or LinkedIn, or they might be ways you can connect in person.

- How can you be more unique with your products and services? Sit down with a group of friends and brainstorm a list of ways that you can differentiate yourself from your competition.

- Take some quiet time alone to think through what you're currently doing for a living. Do you have a passion for it? If you don't, figure out a plan to get out of that industry in the next year and into what you have a passion for doing.

2

Jack Morgan:
The Christian Martial Artist

My sister called me: "I know you're working on that book—you know, the one you call MO!? Well, I have somebody you have to interview: he is absolutely amazing, and his name is Jack Morgan." I asked her what was amazing about him. She said, "Well, lots of things. He is a wonderful father, a wonderful husband, and a very accomplished man. What really blew my mind, however, is he is in my martial arts class, and he only has one leg." (Silence at the other end of the line.) "Maybe I misunderstood you," I said. "Did you say he only has one leg?" "Yes, one real leg and a titanium one. Let me tell you, martial arts is hard enough with two legs, much less one!"

I called Jack Morgan a few days later to arrange a time to interview him by phone. There were two things he said that were interesting: first, he had no idea why anybody would think of him as special or unique, and second, he said it would be a shame if his wife was not in the interview with him. "My wife is heavily involved in everything I do, and I couldn't have done anything without her." A few days later, I interviewed Jack and Lora Morgan, and the story that unfolded was amazing.

Jack Morgan grew up in a typical Southern family in Wyoming County, West Virginia, in the southern part of the state. His father was a coal miner and a minister at the Church of God. It was a solid blue-collar family raised on wholesome values, and though their family struggled financially, his father always refused social help. He was proud and did not believe in handouts. At eighteen years old, Jack decided to see the world and joined the Air Force for four years. Jack came back from the Air Force. Afterward, he started attending college. Lora was attending Bluefield State College, and Jack would cruise into town on Friday nights in his hot rod. It being a small town, all the kids would cruise on Friday and Saturday nights. That's what they did. Lora's friend happened to be dating Jack's cousin, and that's how Jack and Lora met. Jack would always remember the date they first met, March 17, because Lora changed his life. In fact, they came to celebrate this day more than their actual wedding date. Jack laughingly describes their first date as a one-on-one basketball game.

They were married on October 12, 1991, and they became the typical happy young married couple. They were also very active in their church, and after a few years they decided to move to Virginia to work in the Presbyterian Children's Home of the Highlands. They both worked there for three years and had a wonderful time traveling around the southeast camping, hiking, and getting to know one another.

Eventually, they decided to leave the Home of the Highlands. They wanted to have children, but they didn't have much money, so Jack went to work for a large lighting company. Life was good and they had a son in 1999 and a daughter in 2006. Jack eventually decided to quit his regular job to start his own electrical contracting company, and for the first six months, things were going well.

Then Jack and Lora's church planned to move into a new church building, and they found out about a theater in another town that was willing to give away its old seating. Jack teamed up with a few teenage boys and young men to go and pick up the chairs. On a dark morning with a light snow, he left the house. As he was leaving, Lora asked him to wait a few hours until the snow cleared and it was lighter outside. Jack pressed on though, for he had an important task and he wanted to get it done. As Jack and his team of young men and teenagers were traveling down Highway 81 toward Blacksburg, Virginia, they witnessed an accident. "It was strange," says Jack. "We actually watched the accident as it happened." He was concerned that people may have been injured, so he pulled over. It was 6:30 a.m. when he got out of his truck. He called 911 and told them about the accident. As he approached the accident site, checking on a car, he saw a young man running down the road and calmed him down. There was a debris field of wreckage across the road, and Jack was afraid the debris would cause even more people to crash. Jogging back to his truck, he pulled out his cell phone and called 911 again and said, "You need to get somebody out here quick; this is going to be bad."

Suddenly Jack's world tilted—he heard screeching sounds and the crunching of metal, and a car hit him, pinning him to the silver guardrail. He saw the front end of a Chevy lifting up and arching over him through the air. It flew over him, landed, and ran into his own truck. It was a pinball pattern of vehicles flying all over the road, and Jack was in the middle of the action, which ended up being a ten-car pileup. Then Jack went flying straight up through the air. "This sounds weird," says Jack, "but the split second before it happened I knew it was going to." His cell phone flew out of his hand, and the impact was so violent it knocked his body out of his boots and out of his pants. He flew off the side of Highway 81—thirty-five feet into a gully below. He vividly remembers crying out to God as he was flying through the air. When he finally rolled to the bottom of the hill, he was sitting up, his legs under him. When he reached for his left leg, he realized that just below the knee it was gone. He was bleeding profusely and could feel his heart beating and actually see each heartbeat. His right leg was also hurt and possibly broken—but it was there. Since no one knew where he had landed, he had to do a slow and painful climb back up the hill to get help, dragging his body up the incline with his arms, one bad leg, and the stump of his left leg. He remembers calmly praying:

"God, I need your help." Once Jack got back up to the side of the road, he yelled for the boys from his church. One young boy, Chad, was freaked out by the blood and by the fact that Jack's leg was missing. Jack grabbed Chad by the collar and said, "You have thirty seconds to save my life—put a tourniquet on my leg now!" As it turns out, he was right: experts later said he only had two minutes from the time his leg was severed before he would have bled to death. The boys came back with a sweatshirt and tied it around his leg as a tourniquet. Jack realized it was not enough. "Get me a belt!" Someone volunteered a belt. That slowed the bleeding enough. Jack lay on the cold ground on the side of Highway 81, with his left leg somewhere over the guardrail. He gently asked Chad if he would pray with him, and he did. As they waited for an ambulance, Jack said he knew he was not going to die. He felt a comforting physical presence, and had no fear. He believes that this was the presence of God. He said his only concern at that point was how he would live life as before and take care of his family and his business.

As Jack was being loaded into the ambulance, he asked Chad to call Lora and tell her he was OK, but she needed to come to the hospital. At that time, Lora was spending her morning getting ready to host an in-home jewelry party, and their son was next door with his grandparents. The phone rang, and it was Chad. Lora asked, "What happened?" Chad was young and scared and blurted out, "He was in an accident and hurt his leg." When Lora asked to speak to Jack, Chad hung up, and the line went dead. Lora tried to contact their pastor but was unable to do so. A few moments later, the pastor called and told Lora he was heading to the hospital. Lora said she was trying to call Chad, but he wouldn't answer his phone. The pastor promised that he would call Lora as soon as he got there. Lora jumped in the car and headed to the hospital as well. Finally, the pastor called back and said, "Lora it's pretty bad—Jack might lose his leg."

On the way to the hospital, the paramedics in the ambulance almost lost him; he was fighting for his life due to loss of blood. Lora arrived at the hospital where she was met by her pastor who told her they were working on Jack. She asked to see him and the staff refused as they were treating him in the back. At this point, Lora attempted to go through the window, and her determination led them to change their mind. They let her go back to see him. A team of medical people surrounded Jack. Everyone was panicky, but Jack was calm. He lay there, white as a sheet, and somehow through all the people around him, he got a glimpse of Lora and said, "That is my wife." The people parted so Lora could see Jack, and Jack smiled at her and said, "Happy anniversary, baby—it's March 17!" Jack's pelvis was broken and he could barely move. The trauma team wanted to fly him to a trauma center in Roanoke, Virginia, but the weather would not allow it. He was still very unstable, and many people did not expect him to live. A surgeon cauterized Jack's leg, which was intensely painful—but it stopped the bleeding. He got Jack stabilized, got IVs going, and then Jack was ready to be moved to Roanoke. Lora called Jack's parents, telling them what had happened and suggesting that they meet her at the hospital in Roanoke. The medical team in Roanoke looked at Jack's condition and immediately rushed him into surgery, concerned about internal bleeding. While Jack was being prepped for surgery, the team brought Lora some paperwork and said they were not sure if Jack was going to live due to his internal injuries. They asked for her permission to put him on a ventilator if it was necessary. They then informed her that he would be in severe pain after the surgery and would be in the intensive-care unit for several days afterwards. She calmly looked up at the doctor and said, "I rebuke that in Jesus' name." The doctor walked away, shaking his head.

Jack survived the surgery, surpassing all expectations, and the doctor had him cleaned and sewn up. He warned Lora that Jack might not be able to talk for several days. He also stated, "The biggest issue now really is all about attitude."

Jack woke up from his surgery and immediately started joking around with the nurses. He never needed to be intubated, skipped intensive care, and went straight to a private room. He wanted food on the first night, and the staff told him it was too soon to eat. When the doctor checked on him later, he was stunned that Jack was so alert and said, "There's really no way we should be talking." Jack said, "You do what you need to do, and I will do what I need to do, and we'll leave the rest up to God" All the medical staff had predicted Jack would be in the hospital twelve to thirteen weeks. He had all three of his surgeries in the first week and went home after twelve days. They said he might be walking within one year, and he defied the odds by walking within four months. "People have always told me what I should do, but I never really listened to that. I guess I'm always pushing myself to the limit." When he first went to visit the technician who would be working on his prosthetic the technician took one look at Jack and said, "I can tell you you're going to be fine—I can always tell, and you are one of them!" Jack says he guesses the technician was right.

While Jack was in the hospital, Lora was very worried about their finances during his recovery. One late night in the hospital room, Lora whispered to Jack, "Honey, people are giving us money—and it feels uncomfortable and I don't know what to do with it." Jack chuckled, "Well, just use it for whatever we need to use it for." Lora's eyes got really big, "I don't think you understand." She pulled out the money and laid it gently across the bed, and they counted it. They had received over five thousand dollars in the first two days. They were both completely stunned by the level of generosity in their church and the community. Somehow their story ended up on the radio, in the newspaper, and on television. Money came rolling in. "It was amazing," says Jack. "We had people sending us checks who we did not know; we had people coming to our door and giving us cash with tears in their eyes. We had always heard that no one wants to ever help anyone else. Well, it wasn't true in our case." The funny thing is, you know God was in it because they never had to ask for help, and when they no longer needed it, the help stopped.

Jack's philosophy is that when something bad happens you can either accept it, or lie around and be depressed. "There are many other people in worse shape than me," says Jack. He believes that in any situation, attitude determines your level of excellence. Whenever he sees someone who has an artificial leg, he makes a point of stopping and talking with them and encouraging them. Sometimes he even uses the same phrase that the technician who made his first prosthetic used: "I know you are going to be fine, I can just tell!" He can see the look of hope in their eyes.

Now, Jack says it's not just about being satisfied with making it—it's about pushing further. "It may sound funny, but in some ways losing my leg was a true blessing. It brought Lora and me even closer together, and now I'm doing things I've never done before, and have much more appreciation for life and for pushing myself to the next level." He is hunting, fishing, playing baseball, and enjoying his martial arts classes. He is also proud of his high-tech leg and is much more interested in one that works instead of one that is pretty. "I don't try to hide it," he says. "I am proud of it, and don't you dare feel sorry for me."

Jack and Lora have now formed a ministry and travel around speaking and inspiring others, and Jack is a high-ranking official in the Republican Party of Virginia. "My life has changed, and it has changed for the better."

What an amazing man, father, and husband. I also don't think I would want to face him in a martial arts competition.

MO! Notes

1. **Remember that people feed off of optimism.** When Jack was injured, his optimism actually cheered up members of the medical team. Optimism can have a dramatic impact on life in many more ways than you can imagine.

2. **Live with energy.** When you speak with Jack, he is a very humble and unassuming man. But there is one quality that is always there: energy—a spark. You hear it, you feel it, and you sense it. It is one of the key ingredients of MO!

3. **Find a way.** In many situations, Jack had to figure out a new way of doing common tasks, such as getting dressed in the morning, walking, standing, and sitting, just to name a few. It is up to you not to complain, but to find a way.

4. **Reframe.** You can look at adversity as a liability or as a learning experience. Obviously, Jack Morgan looked at adversity and decided to use it to make him a better man and to embrace life—not less, but more.

5. **Feel good about being noticed.** Before Jack lost his leg, there were times when people did not notice him. Now when walking through the mall in shorts with his titanium leg, everyone notices him. Jack has decided that it's OK for them to look, to stare, and to ask questions. There really is not a downside to people noticing you unless you allow it to make you feel bad.

meMO!

- Take out a piece of paper and, on a scale of one to ten, rank yourself as an optimist with the number ten being the best. If your number is below a six, figure out what you can do to be a more optimistic person daily.

- Think about what is limiting you in your life, whether physically, mentally, or spiritually. Take out your calendar, and write down specific activities you can do every day in order to reduce some of these limitations or work around them.

- The quality of your life will definitely be affected by the quality of your team. Look around you in your life, and make sure that you are surrounded by people who will be your advocates. If you honestly and truly believe these people will not be your advocates, then you probably need to surround yourself with different people.

- Make it a goal to try to encourage at least one other person each day who may be going through some trials and tribulations that you have experienced. Take a few moments to help them. It may be an e-mail, a lunch, or a quick phone call that can make all the difference in the world.

3

Vern Oscarson: Fish Peddler Extraordinaire

In any coastal area, there are a lot of places to buy fish. A ton of them, in fact. So it's no surprise that South Florida is the same. In the Fort Lauderdale/Miami region, fishing is a huge industry. There are thousands of professionals and amateurs catching and selling fish and other seafood. Most fish markets are all the same, at least to the untrained eye. However, even with all the places to shop, there are many customers who only go to one place to buy seafood and won't take their business anywhere else. That place is Fish Peddler East, located in Fort Lauderdale, Florida. Why? Aren't they all the same? What is this place's secret weapon?

Simply put, it is Vern Oscarson. If you speak to the store's owner, Vern Oscarson, you would know right away he is the Fish Peddler East, for his passion, drive, and charisma are magnetic.

Vern loves what he does. He has a passion for the business. It's evident in the way that he speaks about his trade. He has a twinkle in his eye. You can also tell by how amazingly neat and clean he keeps his market. It's visible in how carefully he prepares the fish, like a work of art. Most of all, it is obvious that Vern loves what he does when you learn about how hard he's worked to get to where he is today. He earned it. There is no silver spoon in this man's mouth.

Originally from Wisconsin, Vern's family moved to Fort Lauderdale in 1969. As luck would have it, his school, Fort Lauderdale High, just happened to be across the street from a restaurant, the Sea Grille. He started working there part-time, and before he knew it, he ended up in the kitchen. "I think I started peeling shrimp," he recalls, smiling. The longer he worked there, the more he learned about the business.

Vern enrolled in college, and met his future wife two years later. As he puts it, "College went to the wayside, and we started building a life." Seafood was what he knew, so he continued to learn more about it while gaining work experience, so much so that he became the assistant kitchen manager of the Sea Grille.

During his eight years or so in the restaurant business, he met various sellers who supplied the fish to the restaurants. He didn't know it, but he was building his knowledge for the future. One of these sellers was a man named Paul Smith who owned a market called Pop's Fish Market in Deerfield Beach. Vern began working at the fish market part-time, which eventually became his full-time job.

While still in the seafood business, the retail seafood and restaurant seafood industries were quite different, as Vern had been learning. He was amazed by the differences and the subtleties involved. He explains, "Now, you're not cooking your seafood dinner for somebody, you're supplying them with the raw materials for them to cook their own dinners... Being in the restaurant side of the business, you were familiar with purveyors of already-processed products which come through the back door. And then when you get into a retail fish market, which is dealing with the boats, the direct source, it's a completely different animal." Soon Vern was head over heels in love (or maybe fin over tail) with the fish market business.

One day, Vern visited a store called the Fish Peddler, which he found to be very impressive. The products were of high quality, the absolute best that could be sold. Customer service was of utmost importance; if a customer needed anything, the Fish Peddler's employees would do whatever they could to provide it to them. They treated customers like friends and family, not merely like customers. Vern also liked the feel of the store, which had a "comfortable, friendly, almost seaside atmosphere to shop in." Vern began working at the Fish Peddler, originally being hired as the assistant to the general manager. He later became the general manager, and when the Fish Peddler's owners retired, he found investors and bought the business in 1996. That is when he was able to put his personal stamp on the market, keeping all the positives and making it even better.

So why won't customers buy their seafood anywhere else? Of course, the quality of the food is one of the reasons. The biggest reason, however, is the people who work there. Vern trains them to be in tune with the customer and what they want. He also strives to not only sell seafood but also to educate customers about their food and give suggestions on how to prepare it. Would this ever happen in the fish department at a giant grocery store? Nope. Grocery store employees don't have the time, and they wouldn't expend the extra energy it takes. People also like to shop at Vern's store because they become familiar and comfortable with the employees. Because they're happy working there, employees stay at Fish Peddler East for a long time. In a world of "Big Box" stores, Vern has built a small, warm neighborhood market. It's the kind we all miss from our childhood, when everybody knew everyone, and we were all connected somehow.

Employees love Vern and love working for him. Anyone would be fortunate to work for someone like Vern. He has learned, through previous employers, how to (and how not to) treat the people he hires. He believes a positive attitude yields positive results, and people should be compensated for their work. "If someone is capable of doing a job," he explains, "they should be paid well for doing that job, and they'll flourish." This is an interesting concept in the fast-food, minimum wage marketplace. Vern likes to hire people and train them, especially kids, to "give them a chance." He trains them in all aspects of the business. No, there is no specialization here. Vern wants them to understand the business inside and out, the way he learned it. So how does he know whom to promote? His answer is remarkably simple, yet very wise. "If somebody does a spectacular job washing dishes," he explains, "chances are, they'll do a spectacular job at the next level up." He also possesses what is an unusual quality these days: loyalty. He is very loyal. The general manager that he worked with at the Fish Peddler is now the general manager at Fish Peddler East. And the man who hired Vern at the Sea Grille when he was seventeen now works for Vern as well. Huh? So the employee is now the boss, and the boss is the employee? That is called loyalty! The kids these days call something from the past "old school," and this can be an insult or a criticism. But in Vern's case, no one would ever use that as a criticism. They would say that old-fashioned values like hard work, commitment to customers, and paying people well for their hard work are novel ideas. In the age of fast-food and low pay, poor customer service and lack of loyalty on both the part of employers and employees, maybe—just maybe—Vern has something there that is special. Maybe by looking back, it can help us look forward, to perhaps some new models of how to thrive in business.

As we walk away from the market, Vern is educating a customer on exactly the best way to fix and prepare a lovely, bright red snapper. You get the distinct feeling this is something he will never retire from.

MO! Notes

1. **Be loyal.** Vern is so loyal he hires people who used to hire him. In today's world where we

lack connection and stability, loyalty can go a long way. So how can you follow his lead and be more loyal to your professional contacts, your family, and your friends?

2. **Be passionate.** No matter what business you are in, be passionate about it. Yes, people could thumb their nose and say "eww—fish?" but what about being the best? What about being world class? How can your passion make a difference for you as an employee? With Vern, it gets you promoted. The same applies everywhere else too. How can passion make a difference if you are a leader? How can it make a difference if you own a business?

3. **Train them.** Wow! Training people—what a concept! You mean they shouldn't just figure it out on their own? In Vern's own words, "Give people a chance," and train them in all aspects of the business. We have been in the training and development industry a long time. We have seen with our own eyes the remarkable difference it makes when people get development. What can you do to train someone around you?

4. **Learn the business.** You saw that Vern spent many years learning about seafood in both the retail and restaurant arenas. At some point, he became an expert. Strive to learn everything about your business. Read, study, follow the trade magazines of your industry, and go to shows and events. Apprentice, get mentored,

get education and training, and gain experience. We see too many people who want to
be vice president in a few short years without
understanding the ins and outs of their respective business. Create an individual learning
plan for yourself to learn your business.

meMO!

- Be proud to show your passion and your
  loyalty to others and your profession. Declare
  in public for all to hear that you love what
  you do, and explain why you do it. Practice
  doing this at least once a week to someone
  who might not have the loyalty they need
  to make your company one that all will be
  proud of. This can be motivational, and it can
  fundamentally change the attitude of all the
  folks that you work with in your company.

- Be ferocious and persistent about *learning*.
  Make a list of three things you want to learn
  or be better at. Be specific as to when you
  want to have accomplished each goal. Go
  to the Internet or the Yellow Pages and find
  someone who offers the education you want,
  and sign up for the first available opportunity.
  Complete it and move on to the next one on
  your list.

- Be ferocious and persistent about *training*,
  especially if you are a leader in your company.
  Plan yearly what each area or department of
  your company needs to be trained on, and
  train them. In the planning process, ask the

teams of people in each department what training they think they need. This may surprise you. Sometimes what they think they need and what you think they need are different. Take what you learn from this and find a professional to do the training. Find someone who is a great communicator even if they are not an expert in your field. A professional trainer can learn the details they will need to know about your company and its needs. Investing in a true professional is well worth it!

4

Liz Trotter:
The American Maid
Champion

The first things that strike you when you meet Liz Trotter are her energetic eyes, her huge, white smile, her very stylish spiky hair, and the very smart glasses that look like something that an evening news anchor would wear. She smiles almost as if she is keeping a secret, and maybe she is; after all, she has one of the most successful cleaning companies in the Olympia, Washington, area. Few people would realize that she has built her cleaning company from nothing into a million-dollar business.

A person could almost assume that she was born to a very privileged and wealthy family, but that would be the furthest thing from the truth—and a joke to Liz Trotter. Actually, Liz has experienced a great deal of adversity and tragedy in her life, and the fact that she has been able to overcome it all is a testament to her iron will and tenacity.

When the lid of Liz Trotter's life is lifted, it reveals a very tough childhood, although Liz doesn't necessarily see it that way. For her, it was just a stepping stone to the life she's created for herself today. When Liz was very young, her mom was really struggling to take care of her children, and she could not financially afford to take care of them, so she sent them to an orphanage. Later on, around the age of nine, Liz's father came and rescued them from the orphanage and brought them to live with him and his wife. While this sounds like a happy ending, it was actually the beginning of a long nightmare. Liz's father worked full-time and her stepmother worked two jobs, which meant that Liz, the oldest of eight kids, was responsible for watching her seven siblings and at the age of eleven became the mother by default.

Her childhood was a series of scenes of both mental and physical abuse. Her father would force the kids to get into the pool in the wintertime when the water was freezing cold to get the leaves off of the bottom. He would then take the long leaf-skimming net and hold their heads underwater if they were not doing a good job to punish them for their lack of work ethic. Liz was punched, kicked, slapped, yelled at, and held responsible for the other children's poor behavior. Her father often would have the kids run around the backyard while sadistically shooting them at close range with a pellet gun. One of Liz's most unpleasant memories is of her father having all the kids line up, then ordering kid number one to take a belt and whip kid number two. If it was not hard enough, kid number one would be punished. Liz never knew if it would be a good day or bad day at home. When you ask Liz how she was able to survive the abuse, she says she knew that "her dad did not hate her; it was just something wrong with him." Despite her abusive home, she graduated high school.

It's no surprise that at the age of seventeen, Liz decided to escape by moving out and living with a boyfriend. Of course, after she moved, she spent a lot of time worrying about the siblings that she had left behind with her father and stepmother. She got pregnant the same year and had a little girl.

One New Year's Eve when her daughter, Kristin, was just old enough to walk, Liz was driving her late model car and one of her brothers was holding baby Kristin on his lap. Going through an intersection, Liz's car got T-boned by a drunk driver, and little Kristin was tragically killed. Liz went through several years of pain and sorrow, but she continually stayed focused on her future, searching for her place in the world. She went to junior college for a little while, went to beauty school but dropped out without completing it, slept on a friend's couch, and was even homeless for a short time. She tried to go back to college again but was just having a hard time finding her passion.

At the age of twenty-two, Liz married her first husband and then moved to Washington State. There, she had another daughter, Shara, and in the ultimate irony, she decided to start a day care in her home watching eight children. As she looks back on it now, she knew nothing about the profession of child care and didn't have any of the proper licenses or certifications to run a proper child care facility, but somehow it fed her soul. After the healing time with so many young children, she realized that she needed a better job—she needed more out of her life. One of the best turns of fortune for her was when she met a business owner, a Korean gentleman by the name of Jin Soo Na, and his family. He owned a series of Korean dry-cleaners called South Sound Cleaners, where Liz got a job. Jin was nice to Liz, and Liz worked very hard and always looked after the business. He became her valuable business mentor. They were the perfect match. Liz was a young, energetic person who worked hard and could understand Jin's heavy Korean accent. She helped him with whatever he wanted in terms of dealing with lawyers, contracts, and bank accounts, and she always got results. A true entrepreneur at heart, Jin Soo Na decided to open a florist with Liz as the manager. Liz says he always asked her the same questions: "How much money it cost? How much money we make?"

Liz was the perfect employee: results-oriented, committed, hard-working, and really not in it for the money. Her philosophy was always that she had enough to do what she needed to do. Coming from a background of scarcity and abuse, having enough was enough; she had learned about acceptance at a very early age. Around that time, her marriage fell apart and she got divorced. Soon, she felt like she had learned as much from her business mentor as she could and was ready to strike out on her own.

When brainstorming about starting a new business, she thought, "Well, I know a lot about cleaning, being the eldest of eight children, and I know a lot about chemicals, having run a dry-cleaner for multiple years, so why not start a cleaning service for homes and offices?" She had an "in" and she was eager for the opportunity.

Liz has always been enthusiastic about learning new things. She's never given up and she's never stopped learning; she's always wanted to be prepared for what the future would bring.

Seventeen years ago, her company American Maid Cleaning was born. With her daughter Shara, her new husband Tim, and their newborn son Gavin, Liz was working sixteen to twenty hours every day, her company started to grow quickly, and she started adding friends and more family members to her staff. Now her very successful company has grown to more than twenty-seven employees.

What really strikes you as a customer is how very unique the American Maid Cleaning company is. The people who do the cleaning are crisply dressed in uniforms, but not the kind that you would expect. They wear basketball jerseys, shorts, and Crocs, all with a beautiful red, white, and blue theme. Each member of the team, instead of having a number on his or her jersey, has a letter, and that's how you know the order each was hired in. So if you have someone come to your house and there is a "C" on his or her jersey, you have met the third employee hired. And the employees are happy—they love their jobs. While cleaning toilets might not make it high on their list of favorite things, working for American Maid Cleaning is something they can feel proud of. It is quite a sight to see the company vehicle pull up to a home and five basketball players jump out and race inside the house to clean, using a mix of sports terms to describe their business. For example, if a client complains because a house is not cleaned well and the team has to go back and re-clean it, that is called a "free throw." The employees are, of course, "team members," and their clients are "fans." This, along with the freshly baked cookies they leave at each newly cleaned home, really gets people's attention. It's original—it's different!

Liz has a goal to expand her cleaning company, perhaps by franchising in the future, and she is even thinking about coaching other cleaning companies on how to build their business. Most people would wonder why Liz is able to be successful despite her upbringing of physical and mental abuse. When asked, she says, "It is actually fairly simple. I did not want to have that kind of life because it was icky." (I laughed when she said this.) She then told me that she wanted to make sure that her children were not treated that way and that they would not have to grow up with the scars that she has from her upbringing. She was going to stop the cycle of abuse. Liz says, "I learned early on that my life could be exactly what I wanted it to be, and every day for me is a great day! After all, I was trained by life's experiences. If my car breaks down, I think, 'Oh well, it could be worse—*lots* worse.' With the life

I have lived and experienced, I know what worse looks like!" Being remarried to a wonderful man for the last sixteen years has helped Liz to create the peaceful life she craved in her youth. Liz lives her life today as she always has—as an optimist. She says to herself, "I'm looking forward to what is coming, because something great is right on the horizon!" Looking at the future has always made any problems seem small, regardless of the circumstances surrounding her life.

Liz says that her employees are weirdly loyal to her. When asked why, she states very simply, "We just accept our people, and I think they can feel that." (Besides, who wouldn't want to wear cool uniforms like that?) She makes a point to learn about her employees and to understand them—to treat them like a family and to help them feel accepted, because many times they've never felt acceptance in their lives before.

When I asked her if there were any final things that she would like to say, she said, "Well, this may sound odd, but I have always been lucky—just completely super lucky. Great things always happen to Liz Trotter."

I couldn't have said it better myself about this amazing woman who radiates MO!

MO! Notes

1. **Be curious.** Liz was always curious about learning the dry-cleaning business, the florist business, and the home cleaning business. Do you maintain an amazing level of curiosity about learning and studying new things?

2. **Try to understand people.** Try as much as possible to understand why people do what they do and say what they say. It doesn't mean you have to agree with them, it's just important to genuinely try to understand them.

3. **Use your fear.** Liz actually used fear as a motivator to keep her moving forward. So if you are fearful, that's OK—just use that fear as energy to drive you forward.

4. **Be tolerant.** Liz is willing to be tolerant about how people are instead of trying to change them; she accepts them in their current state. Because she is willing to do this rather than being judgmental, she gets a different response from people.

5. **Be an optimist.** Many people say, "What is there to be optimistic about?" Liz reminds us not to get stuck in whatever plight we find ourselves in, but to "look forward to what is coming. Something great is right on the horizon."

meMO!

• Write down a list of bad things that happened to you in the past and how they've affected you. Then, beside each of those items, write down that you will *not* allow them to impact your future, and write how you're going to go about making sure of it.

- Create a learning plan for yourself. Many people tell us that their companies do not have training departments—so if that is the case for you, do your own training! Sit down and decide what skills you want to improve, and then create at least one learning action item for each one.

- Try to learn more about human nature and psychology. Pick at least two to three books about psychology to read this year. Books like *Emotional Intelligence* by Daniel Goleman or *The Platinum Rule* by Dr. Tony Alessandra are good examples. Understanding more about human nature will help you get along with people more effectively.

- Think about the types of people for which you have no tolerance, and try to figure out why you don't have tolerance for them. Come up with a plan to have more understanding for each of those kinds of folks. Pick one person per week to work with. Keep in mind that they should not know that you're doing this. They should just feel you're being more tolerant.

5

Carlos Nunez: JM Lexus One-of-a-Kind Service Advisor

Going to your car dealership for a car checkup or a repair is usually like going to the dentist to have half of your teeth pulled, but not if you own a Lexus, live in South Florida, and are lucky enough to have Carlos Nunez as your service advisor. He is so popular, respected, trusted, and loved that many of his customers come in to try to *take him to lunch* or *just hang out with him* for a while even when their car is not being serviced. What is this about? It is all about Carlos!

As I was waiting to interview Carlos, there were five customers also waiting for him. I jokingly said, "It's like JFK Airport in a holding pattern: stacked up and trying to land." One of the customers heard me and replied, "If that were the case, Carlos would bring us a helicopter and we would land first." It *is* all about Carlos.

It is evident from the moment you meet Carlos that he is a passionate, energetic, knowledgeable guy. You feel it in his handshake, see it in his eyes and smile, and hear it in his words and tone—he loves and cares about what he does and cannot wait to help you through your service appointment or issue. You also get the feeling that Carlos would be great at anything he chose to do in life.

Born in Brooklyn, New York, from Puerto Rican born parents, Carlos, his sister, and his three brothers (one adopted) had to go to work at early ages. Their parents were factory workers earning fifty dollars a month, and everyone had to help out to make ends meet. At age eleven, Carlos was working unloading trucks to earn enough money to buy sneakers. He then worked cleaning a grocery store at night: washing the floor, stocking shelves, and setting up displays. He loved it and took great pride in it.

During summers Carlos also worked for the local police in the community affairs department, taking poor, underprivileged kids on outings and vacations out of the city. He continued to work throughout his childhood and started going to college. After five years, Carlos graduated from Queens College, the first ever college graduate in his family.

Carlos learned from his father that "good things happen to people who work hard," and that lesson stays with him today. With four kids, earning fifty dollars a month, his parents paid off their home in Brooklyn in just eleven years!

After Carlos graduated from Queens College, a friend moved to South Florida and suggested Carlos would love it and should come on down, so Carlos did.

Within ten days, he had an apartment, a car, and a job working for Enterprise Rent-A-Car as a rental agent. He learned he had a gift for talking to people, and he used his ability to develop business with local body shops and dealerships. He quickly became the manager. Carlos developed relationships with his customers, buying them donuts and coffee or lunch, and playing softball with them on weekends. He liked to talk to people, make them feel good, and fix their problems. Eventually he was promoted to a vice president and was moved back to New York.

Carlos missed his wife and two children of six and seven years old, so he left the position and moved back to Florida. He landed a sales job for a construction company, where he once again used his skills and enthusiasm along with his ability to build strong relationships.

Through a friend, Carlos heard about a rental manager position for Toyota Rental Car Company based at JM Lexus. This was where Lexus customers would come to get a rental/loaner car while their car was being serviced. Having experience in this field, Carlos interviewed for the job, landed it, was given a car and double his previous salary, and started the next day. Six months later, unfortunately, the rental car company took this location under their own ownership, and Carlos was out of a job.

JM Lexus saw and heard that Carlos Nunez had great relationships with the Lexus customers who were getting rental/loaner cars, and they offered him a position at JM Lexus as a customer service adviser. He is still happily in this position today after sixteen years, even after being offered many opportunities to become a manager.

Carlos knows that people like to be around happy people. He believes in helping his customers and giving them what they need. He loves the challenge of fixing a problem. When asked what lessons he would teach young people going into business today, he says, "Treat people like you want to be treated: be honest, be ethical, look them in the eyes, tell the truth. Think about the customer before yourself. Prioritize what the customer needs and the other stuff will come later. Be flexible and open to change, and do not let that effect your job." When some coworkers were complaining one day after Hurricane Ike caused all the main Lexus computers to go down, causing lost communication and business, Carlos said, "We just have to work smarter and harder to make up what we lost, and it could be worse: we could have worked at the Lexus dealership in Galveston, Texas, where the hurricane destroyed their homes, business...everything." Even with pay cuts in these hard economic times, Carlos has never earned less; he has just worked smarter and harder to make up for it. He follows the example of his immigrant parents.

Carlos is a positive, high-energy person with great radar. He does not take what he does for granted. Customers are *it* for him. They are what make him a success. He often tells his coworkers, "I am not here to be your friend, even though that would be nice. I am here to take care of my customers and to satisfy my bosses." He looks at his job as if he has five mortgages to pay: his own and those of the four technicians that depend on him to come to work every day. He has had only two sick days in fifteen years. He often visits his customers in the hospital and attends funerals. He cares!

Carlos has a line of fifteen customers after he goes on vacation for a few days, because his customers wait for him. He is a happy guy who loves his job, makes it fun, and at the same time takes what he does very seriously. Good things do happen to people who work hard!

MO! Notes

1. **Be passionate.** Be passionate about what you do and how you do it. If you are going to do a job, do it with every ounce of passion and energy you can muster. Show others how much you love what you do. They will notice it. Customers want to go to someone who is passionate about what they do. Usually passion and confidence translates as "competence" to a customer. Ever notice that in a retail store, the person busy talking, selling, or just putting away stock is the one customers go to for answers to their questions—even if it is, "Where is the restroom?"

Passion is also infectious; you *can* change the other folks you work with.

2. **Give respect.** Respect what you do, how you do it, and the people with whom you do it. Be respectful to others: coworkers, bosses, and customers. When you give respect and show that you respect others and your company by doing a great job, good relationships are built. Good relationships are lasting. The folks you have lasting relationships with will bring others to you.

3. **Work hard and smart.** Nothing in life comes easy. Work hard and smart at whatever you do. No matter how you look at it, it takes work, hard work, and consistency in that hard work, as well as working smart, to make a difference in your job. Carlos and his father are proof that good things do happen to people who work hard and smart.

4. **Relocate.** Sometimes you will need to relocate for a new opportunity. Being open to relocation is also a great message to employers that you are willing to do what it takes for the job. It also shows that you are flexible and a reasonable risk taker—both good qualities.

5. **Look at the big picture.** Like Carlos, think about the others that you work with and how what you do affects them. Be conscious of how you may affect their performance, their work load, and how eventually they, in turn, may affect you.

meMO!

- Find out what you are passionate about in your job and focus on it. Every day and in every way, use this passion to propel you in your daily job, and your passion will most certainly affect others.

- Have a daily plan. Decide based on your workload what your actions will be, staying true to your job and the people you interface with. Showing and giving respect is contagious.

- Every day, pick the three tasks that you need to get done first, and focus, focus, focus on them until they are completed. Begin these tasks with vigor, and put your heart and soul into them until they are completed. You will find that if you work in this way, you will probably end up enjoying many tasks that you previously thought you would not.

- Pick one person in your life that you have the utmost respect for and emulate him or her. Focus on what this person does and the how he or she does it. Start with one characteristic and copy it for a week. Then the next week, add another characteristic you wish to emulate, and work on both. Keep going week by week until you possess all the same good qualities as the person you respect. If these characteristics work for one person, they can work for *you*.

- When being interviewed, make it clear to the interviewer what you are willing to do to get the position (e.g., relocate, commute, travel, work from home). Being clear with the interviewer also shows that you are a good communicator. Statistics tell us that people who communicate well are more likely to get a job than people who do not.

CHAPTER

Bill Staton:
The Amazing
Maintenance Man

I was staying at a hotel in Durham, North Carolina, when the air conditioning in my room started making a horrible racket. At around eight o'clock in the evening, I decided that I needed to call the front desk to get the air conditioner fixed, otherwise I was going to have a long night. I was so glad that I did call the front desk, as I was able to meet an amazing man named Bill Staton. There is no question that Bill possesses all the qualities of MO! He is MOtivated, has MOmentum, and certainly has MOxie.

When Bill first knocked on my door, I opened it and he said, "Good evening, sir." He was crisply dressed in his maintenance uniform and was also wearing a big, bright smile. As soon as he arrived in my room, I immediately knew I was talking to someone special. He treated me like an honored guest in someone's home.

He carefully took the vent cover off the air conditioning unit and shined his flashlight in to see what was causing the racket. As he was doing his work, standing on a small stepladder, he engaged me in a lively conversation. When he asked what I did for a living, I told him that I was a professional speaker. "Wow," he said, "that is really something. That is something that I have always been interested in myself." He then asked why I was in town, to whom I was speaking, and what my topic was the next day. He listened with a careful ear, not attempting to respond too much, just kind of taking it all in. He was tall, lean, fit, and had beautiful walnut-colored skin. I knew he was older, but he looked much younger. He had an energy.

"Well," he said, "I think I have this all figured out, and I know what is causing the problem." He tinkered around for a while, made some adjustments, and turned the air conditioner back on. It kicked on quietly, and he reached up and covered the vent with a piece of paper. "What is that for?" I asked curiously. He said, "Well, I can't have this air conditioner blowing oil all over your room, now can I?" This was followed by a big smile. Once the air conditioner seemed to be behaving itself, he removed the paper and white particles flew out of the vent and onto the carpet and the top of the dresser. He sighed. "Well, that won't do.

I kind of had a feeling that was going to happen. I'll be right back, if you don't mind."

Once he left the room, I realized the air conditioning system was purring like a quiet kitten. A few moments later, there was another polite knock at my room door. "OK," Bill said. "Let's see if we can get you fixed up." In one hand he had a vacuum cleaner and in the other hand he had a soft rag and some cleaner. I watched him as he meticulously vacuumed every speck of foreign dust off the carpet and carefully wiped off the surface of my desk and dresser. "You don't really need to do all that," I said. He looked up and smiled, taking pride in his work. "Now—you are a guest in our hotel. Here is the way I see it. Probably sometime later you're going to want to kick off your shoes and walk around the room. I don't want you to have to have white stuff all over your nice black socks." I thanked him for his extra effort.

He told me that the year before he had thirty-nine positive comment cards filled out on him. Keep in mind, he does not work at the front desk or the restaurant, nor is he a bellman. He is simply a maintenance man. But he's actually much more than that: he's a maintenance man with a keen eye for detail and an amazing awareness about customer service and treating people with respect.

"Thank you for fixing that, Bill," I said. "I am sure I will sleep better tonight. I noticed earlier you had mentioned an interest in public speaking, what did that mean, if I may ask?"

"Well," he said, "my life is quite a story, and it has been a lot of ups and downs. But I would like to share my story and speeches and books, because I think it would help young people a lot." We sat and talked for more than thirty minutes like long-lost friends, and his story was amazing.

Born in 1955, Bill grew up on the very rough and tough streets of Harlem, New York. It was a hard-scrabble life. Bill's father was nowhere around, and Bill's mother, who dropped out of school in the eighth grade, was an alcoholic on public assistance. At a very young age, Bill, being the oldest, became the guardian and protector of his two younger sisters Lynetta and Lisa and his brother Eric. All the folks in the neighborhood started calling him "little man," because he was the one who had to take care of his family. Although he is not proud to admit it, there were times in his teenage years when he had to steal or even sell marijuana in order to feed his family. For Bill, it was always about the love of his family. "You know," Bill says philosophically, "sometimes I was so tired and worn-out I just had to leave it up to God. I thought that he would take care of us as I was always trying to do the right thing taking care of my family. I am sometimes embarrassed about what I had to do, but I had to do it."

Despite all his family's difficulties, Bill still managed to make time to play on his high school basketball team, and his dream was to play at the professional level. He knew he was going to go to college. He didn't know how he was going to make it happen, because he did not have the money, but he just knew. Because

Bill had MO!, he just made it happen. A former shop teacher from his high school was able to get Bill a basketball scholarship at New England College. All Bill had to do was pay for room and board and keep his grades up. It was a dream come true for a kid who had talent and motivation. Things went great in the first year and Bill was really enjoying college. At the end of the year, however, a letter arrived from his mother that changed the course of his life.

In the letter, his mother outlined that she was struggling, his brothers and sisters were all staying in different places, they had no money, and if he did not come back and take care of things, the government was going to cut off her welfare. Bill then decided that the family's guardian angel had to go back home, so he dropped out of school. Bill went back to work and landed a job at Montgomery Ward. He worked very hard, starting in the mailroom, and then was promoted to the advertising department and even did occasional modeling. "I have always been a people person," Bill said, "and they can always tell."

Bill married and started a family, and he moved to Atlanta for fifteen years. After getting a divorce, he learned that his mother was battling Alzheimer's disease and moved to Wilson, North Carolina, to take care of her. The move from Georgia and all the expenses of taking care of his mother used up all Bill's savings, and he knew he needed to get a job. Unfortunately, the area where his mom lived did not have much employment. In the same time frame, his car also stopped working and he could not afford to fix it. So he was unemployed and had no car. This did not stop a man like Bill Staton. He decided to use the next best form of transportation: he jumped on his bike. He thought the best jobs were available in the Raleigh-Durham area, so he traveled each day by bicycle, a 120-mile round-trip, to look for work. He would carefully pack a shirt, tie, and slacks in a dry-cleaner bag and put it carefully into a backpack. Once he learned of a job opportunity, he would ride his bike to the location, change clothes in a restroom, and go to the interview. One time a shocked interviewer even said to him, "Didn't I see you earlier riding a bicycle?" When Bill told him yes, the interviewer said, "Now that is a determined man!"

Bill finally landed a job as a maintenance man at the hotel and began riding thirty miles each way to work, five days a week. This meant he needed to leave for work about two hours before his shift started and ride home at midnight in the dark. When I expressed my amazement, he simply said, "You have to do what you have to do."

Bill then shared with me his vision. He has already filed for 501(c) (an official tax category with the IRS for a nonprofit charity) in order to start a charity to build a community center in his area. He has also already started speaking to people about getting grants for these programs and involving Junior Achievement and other neighborhood youth programs for kids to work and start their own businesses. He wants to make a difference in young people's lives so that they can truly achieve their dreams and stay out of trouble and off the streets.

Bill is also starting a small home-based business where he installs carpet, vinyl, and tile in his spare time. He has also started a book about his life experiences called *Angel's Two-Way Street*.

I told Bill that I was writing a book about special people and I would like to include him in one of the chapters. "I would be honored," he said. "Besides, you don't think it was coincidental that your air conditioner happened to be making a racket tonight, did you? We were meant to meet—and it was all planned by a power neither one of us understands." Well said, Bill. Well said.

MO! Notes

1. **Treat others like you treat yourself.** "It's good to be good," Bill says, smiling, and when you treat others better, you can feel even better about yourself. What have you done for someone else lately?

2. **Don't let people bring you down.** People will do you wrong, but don't let them bring you down. If you fall down, get right back up on your bike and just keep going.

3. **Look at life and just get it done.** Too many people say they can't or think they can't. Don't talk about it; just go do it.

4. **Be persistent.** Many people would allow themselves to stay unemployed, saying that they live in the wrong area. Bill did not make that a barrier. When his car broke down, he

did not allow that to stop him; he just jumped on a bike.

meMO!

- We know from our research that less than 3 percent of the population has clear, articulated goals. Take out a piece of paper and a calendar or journal and write down specific goals for your life, both personal and professional. It doesn't matter what time of year you do this; there is no time like the present.

- Identify in advance the barriers that might interfere with your ability to achieve your goals, then think of ways to get around, over, or through those barriers. Now you have goals and a plan.

- Once your goals and plan have been written down, set a timeline for them. Now take the timeline and mark all those dates in your calendar so you can keep track of them.

- How would you describe your overall attitude? If you would not describe your overall attitude as completely 100 percent positive, then you may need to consider changing it. Try to determine what is causing you to have a negative attitude and, most important, what you need to do to change it.

7

Kate Holgate:
The People Magnet

I first met Kate Holgate when I was attending a National Speakers Association conference. She was standing in the middle of the lobby surrounded by people, as if she were somehow a people magnet. After we met, about every five minutes a different person would come over and say hello, give her a hug, and chat with her. She seemed to literally know everyone, and everyone seemed to know her. That is just the kind of person that Kate is, because she has MO!

When I first requested to do an interview with Kate, she said, "Why me?" which illustrates the level of humbleness she possesses. Kate is in every way a "people person." All of us have known someone like this in our lives. They attract people like a magnet, like moths to a light bulb. They make people around them feel loved and appreciated. So how does someone develop this level of magnetism? I was wildly curious to learn her story.

Kate Holgate was born and raised in Charlotte, North Carolina, in what she describes as a regular middle-class family: a mother and father with two kids. Her mother was a copywriter at a large advertising agency, and her father repaired computer-operated equipment for large textile mills. Kate grew up with one older brother, whom she was constantly in conflict with. They were just different. Kate was born an extrovert, and her brother was born an introvert. Furthermore, according to intelligence testing, her brother was a genius. He was put into a special school for gifted children, and he and Kate never attended the same school until high school. What's interesting is that Kate never really minded her brother having special skills and abilities, nor was she jealous of his intelligence. Part of that was due to her wonderful mother. Her mother always made it clear to her that she did not compare Kate and her brother. Once, her mother joked with her, "Bob might be smart, but he is alone, and you have lots of other friends and many other gifts." Kate grew up in a tall family: she was five foot seven by the time she was ten years old. Her mom was six feet tall but always jokingly described herself as five foot twelve.

As with many kids, Kate's first outside influence was a remarkable teacher by the name of Ms. Fitzsimmons, who had been a body double for Maureen O'Sullivan, the actress in the Tarzan movies. She taught

English classes and was quite the personality. At the end of the year when the kids begged her, she actually entertained them by doing a Tarzan yell on the last day. What amazed Kate about Ms. Fitzsimmons, however, was that on the first day of class, she asked Kate if she had any relation to Bob. Kate told her that Bob was her brother. Ms. Fitzsimmons came over to her, saw the look on her face, and said very quietly, "Just remember: *you are you*." That was a great relief to Kate; it made her feel she could be herself and not be compared to her brother.

Growing up, Kate was definitely daddy's girl, and he and Kate did many things together because of her innate curiosity. Her father was a problem solver and a handyman, and if he was repairing the car and Kate walked by and said, "What are you working on?" he would take the time to explain and actually ask her to help. They worked on gardening, mechanics, and all sorts of projects around the house, and her father even taught her archery and let her shoot with the men in competition. It was, early on, a very pleasant childhood with highly supportive parents.

Unfortunately, everything in Kate's family changed when she was twelve, and not for the better. During that time, her father became involved with a religious cult called Garner Ted Armstrong and the World Church. Overnight, he transformed from a laid-back, supportive father to a religious fanatic. Suddenly Kate went from being a good girl to being called a "whore" because she had long hair and had the audacity to wear lip gloss. He would scream and yell at Kate and would even occasionally hit her, reciting Bible verses about how she needed to be saved. Even though

Kate found this tremendously disturbing, she seemed to have a sense that her father had developed a mental illness. To make things even more confusing, however, there were times when her father would revert back to the old father of the past and would be kind, nice, and supportive. Then he would revert back to the fanatic again when something set him off. One can imagine how incredibly confusing this must have been for a twelve-year-old.

Another teacher who had a big impact on Kate was named Mr. Barnhart. Mr. Barnhart once gave Kate an assignment to make a movie about American history. She went to him because she was worried, and she said, "I don't think I can do it." He gave her a steely look and said, "If you *want* to do it, you can do it—so do it." This gave Kate a tremendous boost of confidence, knowing her teacher believed in her. The version of her old father emerged, and he took a great deal of pride in helping her with the film. They edited the film and added the sweet refrains of "America the Beautiful" in the background. He was proud of her work.

Kate entered her high school years as a hippie—classic for that time—with long hair and bell-bottom jeans with an upside-down Felix the Cat patch on the back pocket. She wore Zig Zag shirts and openly admits that she rebelled and started doing lots of drugs. At the age of fifteen, she was suffering from very low self-esteem and attempted to kill herself because she did not know what she did wrong to make her father abandon her. As she described it to me, "I had a Dad who was addicted to religion and a Mom who was addicted to cigarettes." She still wonders how she escaped the addictions that seem to plague her family.

At the age of sixteen, Kate met and married someone in order to escape the house and get away from her father. She married Michael, who was eighteen and worked at a warehouse. They had fun "playing house," did lots of drugs, and were way too immature to actually be married.

Kate's mother was also suffering. The weekend that Kate got married, her mother moved into Kate's old bedroom and not long after separated from Kate's father and divorced him.

Seven years later, Kate discovered that her husband was cheating on her and they also divorced. She had been married and divorced by the age of twenty-three.

In order to get over the pain, she had to be busy doing something, so Kate volunteered to run a local softball league. As luck would have it, at one of the games she met a man named Dick and they fell in love. Dick was clean-cut and athletic, and he asked her to marry him after only ten days. Looking back on it, Kate realizes that she and Dick were not compatible in any way, shape, or form. She realizes now that she married a man that she thought her daddy would love. All Dick was interested in was playing sports and watching sports. He was not very sensitive to Kate's needs. They did, however, get married.

Shortly after that, Kate's mother started her own advertising agency, and she asked Kate to work there as an account manager. Being the consummate people person, it was Kate's dream job. She had the mind to handle the technical accounts (after all, she had learned a lot about technology from her father while she was growing up). Her mother handled the less technical accounts. In many ways, Kate's mother was like her: everybody loved her, she was quite the character, and all the vendors and suppliers loved her. When media representatives came to talk to her about buying advertising, she would take them out to the hallway and roll dice with them for discounts. Everyone loved her. One of the most important lessons that Kate's mother taught her was this: "Do not judge me by my success; judge me by my attempts."

Around this time in her life, Kate sat down for a talk with her father, and he humbly asked her to forgive him for how he treated her all those years of her childhood. He told her that he would take it all back if he could. Ironically, however, he still remained a religious fanatic for the rest of his life.

Kate's mother was diagnosed with lung cancer in August of 1988 and died very quickly in November of the same year. Kate was devastated; she had lost her best friend, business partner, mentor, and mother. She did not know what to do with the rest of her life. She had worked at her mother's company for eight years.

Her marriage had already begun to unravel, and the stress of all that had happened was too much. She knew she could not live her life with a husband who gave her no support.

Shortly after her mother died, Kate was stressed out and grieving, and she got a call from her cousin

Reggie, who invited her to come to Florida to hang out, go to the beach, lie in the sun, and figure out what she wanted to do next. She took him up on his offer and went to the beach to reevaluate her life. A few days after she arrived at Reggie's house, she reconnected with Reggie's brother, Rick, whom she had not seen in twenty years. Rick walked into the house, took one look at Kate, smiled, and said, "Well, Kate, looks like puberty was pretty nice to you." She fell in love on the spot and moved to Sarasota with him eight months later. Rick and Kate have now been married for twenty-one years. Kate laughs when she tells people she married her cousin—whom she calls her "cousband"—saying, "I am Southern, after all!"

Seeking a creative outlet similar to an advertising agency, Kate started working for the Asolo Theater Company and then went to the Florida State University/Asolo Acting Conservatory. After Kate worked there for fourteen years, the school hired a new dean, and he fired her.

In 2004, Kate learned that there was going to be a fundraiser to benefit victims of Hurricane Charlie, and while working on the volunteer committee, she suggested that Linda Larsen, a professional speaker and a graduate of the conservatory, and her husband, a local television meteorologist, MC the event. Talking backstage the evening of the event, Linda asked Kate, "What are you doing lately? I need you to come and work for me." Kate agreed to go to work with Linda. Kate fell in love with the world of professional speakers. She loved every minute of it because she was able to apply all of her skills.

Sadly, Kate had to quit her job and leave town after a few years to take care of her brother, who needed a liver transplant. After she nursed her brother through his illness, she decided to start a business of her own, managing other professional speakers. She was lucky because Linda had taught her everything she knew about the speaking industry, and Kate loved having her own business.

When asked why she does what she does, her answer is straightforward and instant: "I have the best, most perfect job in the world. I get to be around people whom I love and I love working with. I also feel a very strong need to be part of something important. You see, I know that I am part of something important because the speakers that I represent are out there changing the world."

When people learn about Kate's childhood, they tell her they are sorry. Kate, however, is not sorry, because her childhood made her who she is today. Even though she lost her mother, if her mother had not died, Kate would not have reconnected with Rick, gotten a job at the conservatory, met Linda, and been pushed into starting her own business: "You have to push through the stuff in life, because what you learn eventually is that there is a reason why everything happens."

"I am in the groove," says Kate, "and I can't wait to see what tomorrow brings, having a great husband like Rick and wonderful people around me whom I love."

When you talk to Kate on the phone, you can hear the words and, as corny as it may sound, you can also feel the love.

MO! Notes

1. **Accept that stuff happens.** It is not what happens to you that shapes who you are; it's how you react to what happens to you. Kate could have certainly given up when faced with adversity in her life, but she did not—she just kept going.

2. **Work with people you love.** Too many times we choose to work with people who are not positive, not motivated, and not a good influence on our lives. Kate has decided whom she will and will not work with, and that has had a big impact on both her and her work. When she says, "I love my speakers," she really means every one of those words.

3. **Be able to laugh.** Kate has the remarkable ability to laugh and is always joking around. When describing the husband who cheated on her, she said, "He wanted me to share my bed with some other woman—and mama don't play that way!" You just have to laugh at her Southern sense of humor.

4. **Be persistent.** Kate's mom taught her the value of persistence, hard work, and sticking with your dreams. Often we give up too soon.

5. **Have perspective.** Eventually, Kate was wise enough to understand that her father's fanaticism was a form of psychosis, not something that was her fault. She was able to analyze it on a different level.

meMO!

- Make a list of the things that you love about your work. Yes, we said the word *love*, not *like*. If the list of things you love is a significant list—congratulations. If the list of things you love is short, then figure out how you can love more things about your work, or go do something else.

- On the left side of a piece of paper, make a list of all the challenges that you're currently facing in your life. On the right side, list the ways in which other people may see them. This may help you analyze a challenge from a different perspective.

- If you need to develop a better sense of humor, make a list of things you can do this week to make yourself laugh more. It may be watching a funny television show or movie, reading a funny book, or being with funny people.

- Do something new. When people do something new, it often leads them to new discoveries and opportunities. Decide each week on some new social or professional opportunity you can get involved with that will possibly help stimulate your thinking and boost your morale.

- Make a list of people whom you have an impact on socially and professionally. Ask this question to yourself: Have you done anything in the last two to three weeks that had a positive impact on these people? If not, make a deliberate effort this week to have a positive impact on them by taking some sort of action.

Pedro Valente:
Walking the Walk Always

Meeting Pedro Valente is an inspiration. He is a true example of a man that walks the walk and talks the talk every single day.

Pedro and his two brothers Gui and Joaquim own and run the Valente Brothers Jujitsu Academy in Miami, Florida. They are masters of the art of Brazilian Jujitsu and are respectful through and through to the deepest tenets of the discipline.

Pedro shines from within. He stands, with no body fat, in the best posture you have ever seen: feet firmly planted, body well balanced over his hips, and always with a big smile, wearing his pristine white Jujitsu gi (a type of kimono). When you speak with Pedro, he is so nice, so polite, and he has all the proper manners of a true professional, a professor of Brazilian Jujitsu. You can hear both his strength and his peace in his voice, you can feel it in his handshake, and you can see it in his eyes. Pedro is totally focused on his lifelong commitment to Jujitsu in every fiber of his being.

Pedro's mission is to bring the discipline and practices of Jujitsu to as many people as he can through the Valente Brothers Jujitsu Academy and his teachings around the world.

In life, you meet people who do a job, "their job," and after that job is over for the day, they kind of turn into an ordinary person. This is not true of Pedro. I am not saying he is not an ordinary, regular kind of person—I am saying that the ordinary, true person you see in Pedro is who you see during his classes, after his classes, and all the time, 24 hours a day, 7 days a week, 365 days a year. He lives and breathes what he teaches; he walks the walk and talks the talk relentlessly.

Pedro started learning Jujitsu at the age of two in Brazil, where he grew up. Pedro's grandfather, Dr. Syllo Valente, introduced Pedro's father, Pedro Sr., to Jujitsu at the age of nine. Grandfather Syllo was a naturalist, a homeopathic doctor, and an avid admirer of Jujitsu grand master Hélio Gracie. One day he took Pedro Sr. to watch the world title fight between Hélio Gracie and Masahiko Kimura. Syllo and Pedro Sr. were very impressed with Hélio's amazing technique, and decided to enroll at the original Gracie Academy in Rio de Janeiro. Grandfather Syllo knew it was just the right compliment to his life and the education of his son, and so the tradition continued on to Pedro Jr. and his two brothers.

Pedro explains that his last name, Valente, means "brave" in Portuguese. As a young boy growing up in Brazil, his father had to prove the name he carried. Jujitsu provided a powerful tool to cope with bullies, but it was also a source of confidence that gradually taught him alternatives to physical confrontation.

Pedro and his brothers took private lessons from grand master Hélio as soon as they learned to walk. Throughout their training and their childhood, they had the privilege of also learning from each of the seven Gracie Brothers, the sons of grand master Hélio.

Pedro worked hard at Jujitsu, learning the discipline from all perspectives: mind, body, and spirit. At the age of eighteen, Pedro decided to move to the United States to attend the University of Miami School of Business Administration. To prepare him for the challenges of moving to a foreign country and living alone, his father sent him to grand master Hélio's ranch in Itaipava, Brazil. There, Pedro was carefully prepared to live alone in America and trained to introduce the art of Brazilian Jujitsu to Miami.

Pedro received his Instructor Certification from the Gracie Academy and started teaching classes in Miami. While in college, he continued his training through many trips back to the Gracie Academy in Rio de Janeiro. In 1995, he founded a Jujitsu club at the University of Miami, where he taught several students and faculty members.

In 1997, grand master Hélio came to Miami for the first time to teach classes and supervise training. He continued to come to Miami every year until his last international trip in 2007 before his passing two years later at the age of ninety-five. During this time, Pedro continued to teach private and group classes all over Florida. In 1998, with the help of his longtime friend and student James Robertson, Pedro inaugurated his first full-time academy in Sunny Isles, Florida. One year later, Pedro's brother Gui moved to South Florida to attend Barry University and help Pedro with the academy. The addition of Gui helped to accelerate the growth of the academy, which was just the beginning of the great success they would experience. "Gracie Miami" started being known as "Valente Brothers," and it was internationally recognized as the home of the genuine Brazilian Jujitsu of Hélio Gracie in Florida.

Pedro went on to successfully complete the professor's course and receive the title of Jujitsu professor as well as a master's degree in business administration. Not a small feat while running a business that requires hands-on teaching and the extreme discipline that is needed to be a master of Brazilian Jujitsu. Gui followed suit and attained both his Jujitsu professor diploma and a master of science in sport management. Pedro's youngest brother, Joaquim, also has his Jujitsu professor diploma and a degree in criminology from Barry University.

All three Valente Brothers' excellent instructional skills and technical fighting styles allowed them to receive their black belts directly from grand master Hélio Gracie. The honor of receiving the title of Jujitsu professor from grand master Hélio Gracie is in itself remarkable; in seventy-five years, only twenty-seven people received this diploma from the grand master.

Pedro has never had chocolate, coffee, soft drinks, or alcohol. He eats fruits, vegetables, and fish. He is relentlessly dedicated to Jujitsu, and to being the best professor of Jujitsu for his hundreds of students around the world.

The rules Pedro lives by he refers to as "7, 5, 3: The Virtues of a Jujitsu Warrior."

The first are the "Seven Principles of the True Warriors."

1. **Rectitude.** Doing what is right without regard for the consequences

2. **Courage.** Inner strength to resist opposition

3. **Benevolence.** The disposition to be good

4. **Politeness/propriety.** Proper consideration and courtesy to others

5. **Honesty/sincerity.** Genuine integrity in character and action

6. **Honor.** Profound respect and ethical conduct

7. **Loyalty.** Faithfulness and allegiance

    The next are the "Five Keys to Health":

1. Rational nutrition

2. Sensible exercise

3. Efficient rest

4. Proper hygiene

5. Positive attitude

Pedro says, "If you come up short, or miss one, it throws your entire body off—no good"!

Pedro refers to the final three as the "State of Mind a Warrior Should Have":

1. **Zanshin.** This means awareness, alertness, and readiness—the ability to be prepared 24/7. Unlike a boxer, who may train for three months to prepare and get his body ready for a fight, a follower of Jujitsu has no off-season. One is prepared and strong always—strong in any moment, strong in a crisis. It is a lifestyle.

2. **Mushin.** This literally means "no mind." If there is too much on the mind, it slows one down. A clear mind allows one to react spontaneously. Warriors always react with a clear mind.

3. **Fudoshin.** This means a "state of emotional balance." With this, nothing can move one out of the center. One is always at the center of the bell curve. Variations in emotion are small. There is no drama, no sadness when there are difficult events, no depression, no celebration, and no big adrenaline rushes. It is "real balance."

The philosophy of "7, 5, 3" is based on efficiency, maximum effectiveness, and minimum expenditure of energy. It is a conscious effort to live a righteous life and to have the courage to do what *is* right. Pedro says, "Without courage, you cannot be honest." Like the meaning of his last name, Valente, courage, along with generosity, a sense of belonging to the community, and living in the righteous way, strengthens character. You will live longer, have a sense of real purpose, enjoy your friends, and have a meaningful lifestyle in which you will be able to resist outside negativity.

Pedro is constantly sharing this philosophy, what he calls "the secret to a healthy life." He feels so honored to travel all over the world to help people change their lives. He helps people stop destructive habits that are corroding them, like drugs, alcohol, or partying too much. He says, "Any animal, large or small, does four things: sleep, wake up, eliminate, and have sex. To do these four basic things, humans, through our daily behaviors, need antidepressants and sleeping pills to sleep, coffee to wake up, medicine to go to the bathroom, and Viagra. This is an example of what is fundamentally wrong with many peoples' lives."

Brazilian Jujitsu helps to build confidence, courage, strength, balance, peace, patience, understanding of others, and overall good health, with dedicated principles to live by and over five hundred moves to learn. Ultimately, Jujitsu is most often used by its students to stop violence.

I know many people that practice Jujitsu. I know some who have just started studying it over the last few years. Observing the changes and the transformation that Jujitsu has given them, in mind, body, and spirit, has also very much changed me.

MO! Notes

1. **Walk the talk.** If you are going to be the master of something that you teach others, walk, talk, and live by your beliefs.

2. **Have respect for your elders.** Respect for elders, both in private and in public, can change the world, or at least a community.

3. **Manage your life.** If you manage your life well and learn to focus your efforts, you *can* go to school, work, and have success all at the same time.

4. **Remember that you only have one body.** Your body is your temple; treat it well, and be careful what you do to it.

5. **Learn from the best.** It is always wise to learn from a professional, and if possible, try to learn from the best, even if it is through books or videos.

6. **Make sure to exercise.** Exercise (or in this case, a discipline) that creates confidence and physical improvement in the body feels great.

7. **Practice humility.** Humility is a gift.

meMO!

- Be true to yourself in all that you do. Have a talk with yourself every single day. Put it on your calendar and plan some time for it. It can take just one minute a day. Reflect on who you are, what your attributes are, and what you want to accomplish that day and in your life in general. As you grow and change and develop further, your daily reflections will as well.

- Showing respect to all you meet, in all you do, is not hard. You just have to decide to do it. When you catch yourself not being respect-ful, stop, think, and reflect on how it feels to give respect, and move toward that feeling.

- Eat right daily. This is simple to say, but hard for some to do. Make a list of the foods you eat that you know are not best for you. Read over this list every morning and if possible before every meal. Make it a point to avoid as many of these foods as possible. Try to do this every single day for a month. Habits are often built by repetition over a period of time. At the end of the month, even if you did cheat with some meals, you are better than you were before you started.

- Exercise daily. (This is another statement that is simple to say.) Just keep moving. Do some-thing physical every single day, and mix it up. Put the activity you intend to do on your daily to do list, and do it. On Sunday night, plan your activities for the week ahead. Start off with a simple activity like taking a thirty-minute walk, and work up to doing more as you get more fit. Find a friend that you can do this with, and help each other stay with the program.

9

Stephanie Bolton: Just Past the Trees

Many years ago, in a different time and place, there was a flood in Palm Springs, California, when one of the local dams broke.

In the urban area of town, right next door to the golf course, just past the trees, lived an eleven-year-old girl named Stephanie Bolton. She was having her birthday party that day. All her friends were there celebrating her special day, when all of a sudden there was water coming into the yard and then into the house. Stephanie can still remember the panic, the running around, and the sounds of the helicopters overhead that came to rescue the children from her party. She also remembers that they took the white kids first while the rest of them scooped up water with anything they could find, dumping it in the bathtub and sinks to try to stop the water from taking over the house. When the water could not be stopped, they left the house and ran up the block to higher ground, and there they were safe at last. Stephanie remembers her pregnant older cousin escaped the house at the last minute through a window. She also remembers wearing her paper dress and her Ked sneakers for three days until the neighborhood finally got help. Assistance came only after Stephanie's mother called their senator and the local press and the government realized how significant the situation was.

Shortly after the flood, Stephanie went to live in Palm Springs with her grandmother Octavia, her father's mother. Stephanie would go to church almost every single day with her grandmother. Going to church was what her grandmother did; she was a church lady. It was her social outlet, and so Stephanie had to go too. Today, Stephanie is not a very religious person, but she is very spiritual. Grandmother Octavia sang all the time. Stephanie says her grandmother was always a beautiful, positive, loving person, focusing on God through prayer and song. This is where Stephanie got her spiritualism and most of her singing MO!

Stephanie was born in Los Angeles, California. At the age of two, she moved with her mother and father to London. Her father, Steve Clark, was a dancer, and that was where the work was. He was one of the Clark Brothers, a song-and-dance duo. They lived in Europe, moved around a little, and had a very adventurous life on the continent. Stephanie started school when they lived in Copenhagen, Denmark. Shortly after, they moved to Palm Springs, where Stephanie and her mother lived with her grandmother Octavia.

When Stephanie was ready to start junior high school, she and her mother moved back to Los Angeles. Her mother was always very supportive of her. Stephanie remembers that her mother would always say, "Stephanie, *you* are wonderful, you can do anything."

In school, Stephanie was very active in theater. She thought theater was going to be her career path. She loved singing and, of course, dancing, which she got from her father. She was an honor student at Dorsey High School in Los Angeles and the homecoming queen. She was also the first black drill team leader, as well as its only black member at the time. She had MOmentum.

Stephanie attended Cal State College and always pursued opportunities for theater and acting. She auditioned for the television show *Good Times* for the role of Thelma, but she did not get it. She knew she was not getting the blocking part of acting. (*Blocking* is the process of planning where, when, and how actors will move about the stage during a performance.) Frustrated by this, and knowing she had the gift of speech, she decided to change her major to communication with a concentration on public relations.

She landed a job with Hertz Corporation as a marketing coordinator for car sales and then worked for Kal Kan, a dog food company, in the sales promotion department. Stephanie finally worked her way back into the theater business with MGM Films Distribution, where she worked in the marketing department.

Her job was to put together the negotiations between theater owners and advertisers. Her gift of speech, her ability to negotiate, and her love of the theater all worked together there.

Along the way she got married, had a son name Stephan Philyaw, and eventually divorced. Raising a son as a single parent, working seemed forever in her future.

She eventually left MGM and moved to Jovet Property Management in Beverly Hills, California, where she did marketing and property management for strip malls. One of her friends worked for *Car and Driver Magazine* and told her about a great job as their marketing manager. Stephanie applied, got the position, and convinced *Car and Driver* to start doing their own marketing to show their clients what they could do for them. It worked!

While at *Car and Driver* she was a "front·man" (a term given to the person or team that goes to an event to set up and get ready for an event), and she was in charge of going to Atlanta for the National Automobile Association show. When she got there, she had to make sure everything was ready, but she could not find the signs that were shipped in for the show. This was a big problem. She used her gift of speech and negotiating skills and finally got a terrific guy there to help her find the signs. The show went on without a hitch and met with great success. But it was a success in another way—Stephanie and the nice guy that helped her find the signs fell in love and got married. His name was Michael Bolton (no, not the singer). Stephanie and her son Stephan moved to Atlanta to live with Michael, where she did various jobs for the Travel and Weather channels, Bellsouth Entertainment, and Bellsouth Tele-communications and eventually switched career paths to teaching.

She loved teaching, especially kindergarten, first and second grade, and, of course, physical education. As Stephanie says, "You get them when they just love you and say things like, 'I just love your neck-a-lice Miss Stephanie.'" She could sing and dance and just have fun with the children.

Teaching gave her time to spend with her son during his high school years, and because she was a teacher, she could go to the games earlier than other parents could to supply the food for the kids. Stephanie was known as "the hot dog mom," always there early and always there with hot dogs, all the way to her son's senior year. I also know that Stephanie was always there singing, dancing, smiling, loving, and showing her spirituality—her MO!

Stephanie's son, Stephan, applied to six colleges and was accepted by all of them. He chose Loyola Marymount University in Los Angeles where he is studying multimedia, distribution, and postproduction.

Stephanie's husband Michael had an opportunity to be transferred to the West Coast. Yippee! They could be closer to Stephan in school! Well, it turned out to be Las Vegas, not Los Angeles, but it was closer to Stephan, so they moved to Las Vegas.

Once they moved to Las Vegas, Stephanie taught for Clark County for a while but really wanted to get back to using her marketing skills. She always thought working for an airline would be fun, so she landed a job with US Airways and Air Tran as a ticket and gate agent. I can just see her, singing and dancing and lighting up the skies before the passengers even board the plane.

Las Vegas at that time was on fire in terms of growth, and she heard about "City Center" and the terrific properties going up there. She landed a position working with all four properties at City Center, marketing and selling the dream of living on the Las Vegas strip. Her main audience to sell to was investment bankers, high rollers, and the like. All of this was being done while the foundation for the properties was just being poured. She loved it.

Stephanie then heard about a position for the MGM Resorts Company at Mandalay Bay for an events and hotel sales person. This was everything she loved to do. She could use her speech, negotiation, planning, and marketing skills, all of it, at this job. She applied, got the position, and ended up as a sales manager and worked there for five years. As Stephanie says, "I love MGM Resort Properties; I drank the Kool-Aid and loved it." "Drinking the Kool-Aid" means buying into the mission, values, and beliefs and really, really getting what a company is all about. Stephanie really, really got it.

I met Stephanie while she was in this position and she was not only terrific and so professional at what she did, but she made me feel so good about life. I remember thinking to myself, *This lady is beautiful, fun, outgoing, and so very full of life.* Her *joie de vivre* (or "love of life," as the French say), her verve, her spirituality, and the way she was always singing and doing a little dance with such energy, all of it, made me and everyone else feel *great!* You just know you have to get to know her, and you want to be around her. And besides that, she is a very professional sales manager, event person, planner, negotiator, and more when it comes to details and getting the job done right. I loved every moment with Stephanie and our event was a smashing success largely due to Stephanie and the wonderful team we worked with.

Recently, Stephanie moved to a new position as regional sales manager with Hilton Grand Vacations in Las Vegas. I know they will never be the same. There will be a lot more fun, singing, dancing, and loving life with Stephanie around.

I used to say this only about my Aunt Palma, but now I can say it also about Stephanie Bolton: she would even have fun buying pork chops in the supermarket—all because she *really* has MO!

What's there not to like?

MO! Notes

1. **Don't hold back.** Remember to sing and dance in public if the spirit moves you. Others might just love it.

2. **Sell.** Selling, negotiating, and marketing skills are made better with energy and enthusiasm. No one wants to deal with a dud.

3. **Be enthusiastic.** Enthusiasm is infectious; use yours.

4. **Learn from your elders.** Learn from your elders' experience and use what is in your genes.

5. **Be flexible.** Keep your eyes open to the next good opportunity. It may change your life. *You* may change someone else's.

6. **Put your past behind you.** Even if you start life just past the trees, with rising water and paper clothing, you can be someone terrific in this world and change it for the better.

meMO!

- Being enthusiastic and having more energy can be an acquired attribute. You have to work on it. The best way to decide to do this and practice doing it is to think about your day, out in the world, once you leave your home, as "It's Show Time!" Simply decide and act, and be more enthusiastic and exude more energy. Just try it! Do it every day, all the time, and eventually it will become part of you. You may find that you will build up to this over time, so start off slower and then rise to a full throttle.

- Look and listen when opportunity knocks. Listen with your third ear (to what is being said and what is *really* meant by what is being said) for opportunities that come your way. These usually come for a reason. Seize the moment and remember to ask questions. Within two days, take action on the opportunity. Follow up and follow through.

- Stop feeling sorry for your troubles. Look around you and be grateful for what you have, and don't focus on what you don't have. Everyone on this Earth has woes and troubles at one time or another, so get over it and give thanks!

10

Steven Rowell:
The Serial Entrepreneur

When you meet Steven Rowell, you realize that he has the amazing, unique ability to connect with someone almost instantly. And you wonder to yourself, *How did that skill get developed?* When asked, he will tell you that it is a mix of growing up as the underdog and learning the value of compassion.

From a young age, Steven was picked on by bigger kids. He became the underdog. He decided that somehow he was going to make it in life. Growing up, he was always fascinated by what made people tick and what made people unique. He had a built-in desire to have his own business early on as well.

Steven thought like an entrepreneur and decided at fourteen that he needed a job. Without his parent's knowledge or approval, he applied for and landed a job at the Fort Worth Zoo, serving snow cones and cotton candy to tourists. It was hot, sweaty work, which he didn't mind doing. The work was hard and the pay was only $3.10 an hour, however, and the tourists were generally rude. It was rarely a rewarding job. One day he served cotton candy to a man from New York City, not realizing a bee had accidentally been spun into the cotton candy. The man's wife bit into the cotton candy, the bee stung her, and they became outraged. Thinking that Steven had done this on purpose, the man tried to go through the window of the snow cone stand to attack him. This defining moment made Steven decide that someday, somehow, he would work for himself, make better money, and have more control over his working conditions.

He was lucky enough to have met a great man, a church elder by the name of Will Rogers. From the age of twelve to sixteen, Steven had Will as a mentor. Will gave him lots of sound advice about owning a business and about life in general, and he thought Steven had something special.

At the age of fifteen, Steven decided to start his own lawn-mowing service. (No, that is not a typo; it really does say fifteen.) I asked why he decided to start a business at such a tender age. He said it came naturally to him and just made sense at the time, especially with the mentorship of Will Rogers and encouragement from his own father. Steven went down to the local copy shop and made green flyers advertising his business, S.

R. Lawn Services. By the age of sixteen, Steven's business had grown, and he needed a vehicle to load the mowers in so they could do the work all around Fort Worth. Will Rogers believed in him so highly that he enthusiastically cosigned a loan for a brand-new $6,000 Toyota SR5 pickup truck for a sixteen-year-old. "Will is one of the people that had the biggest impact on my life," says Steven, because "he really believed in me for some reason. He saw a special quality or spark." Steven was also mentored by Walter Naff, his godfather and close friend to his parents, and by Lambuth Tomlinson his 6th grade Sunday school teacher, for whom he is most grateful as well.

Steven was a pioneer in the lawn care business in the Dallas/Fort Worth area because he signed contracts with people, which at the time was not done. He would sell homeowners on the idea that if they signed up for one year (ten months of mowing), then he would give them two fertilizing treatments free during the year. This ended up being a phenomenal success. By the time Steven was a senior in high school, his lawn-mowing and landscaping business employed grown men, and even some of his fellow high school students! Imagine being thirty years old and reporting to a boss who's only seventeen. He left for college, selling the business to another landscaping company in town.

Steven went off to college with a passion for business and an innate curiosity to learn what made people successful. In an organizational communication class, he saw a video with Tom Peters based on the book *In Search of Excellence*. He loved it. This film had a huge impact on his life, and Tom Peters is still to this day one of his heroes. Inspired, Steven decided to learn as much as possible about success from the best source: other people who were already successful. He implemented his "got five minutes?" strategy. He would pick up the phone in his dorm room and dial famous CEOs at various companies, calling the company and asking for the CEO's office. When an administrative person answered the phone, he would say, "Hello, my name is Steven Rowell, and I am a college student at Texas Christian University. I was wondering if Mr. (fill in the blank) would be willing to spend five minutes with me to share the secret to his success." The administrative person would sigh, asking him to hold for one moment, and then go ask the executive if he had five minutes to spend with an ambitious young college student on the phone. Believe it or not, this worked in every case! His first call was with Sam Walton of Walmart for more than one hour; then Fred Smith, founder of FedEx, spent forty-five minutes on the phone with him; and Jack Nordstrom, one of the owners of the Nordstrom chain, spent twenty minutes with him, talking to him from the ladies' shoe department in their store in Chicago! Steven was also able to talk to Red Adair, the world-famous oil rig firefighting magnate; the Bass brothers, Sid, Ed, and Lee, famous for their oil and gas investments; and finally the future president of the United States, George W. Bush.

I asked Steven why he thought these luminaries were willing to spend time with him on the phone. His theory is that these executives were inspired by his question and saw it as an opportunity to give back or share a legacy. They all shared, in their own way, that their children could not care less about what their father did at work, so they apparently were impressed by Steven's ambition and his desire to become successful by learning from their advice. The "got five minutes?" strategy worked so well it boosted his confidence and he learned a lot about business success. He also started to realize there really were no limits to what was possible, and he could start thinking in even bigger scale and scope.

The next giant step in his development was interviewing for the Disney College Program. He still has fond memories of his mother driving him through the snow to the University of North Texas in Denton where the Disney College Program recruiters were interviewing. He could have clearly driven himself, but his mother wanted him to be able to focus and mentally prepare for his interview. He had also sought advice from some of his mentors, so for the Disney interview, he wore a dark charcoal gray suit with a white dress shirt and a red necktie. He also wore a shiny gold Mickey Mouse pin in his lapel. The very first thing Disney recruiter Rick Neely said was, "Steven, you look like you already work for Disney." That was, of course, part of Steven's strategy. Steven ended up working on two different Disney College Program internships during college. While his fellow college interns were out partying and goofing off in the theme parks, Steven was at it again with his "got five minutes?" strategy. Using the Disney Cast Member phone book, Steven made more than 280 phone calls to various Disney animators, executives, engineers, imagineers, directors, producers, and managers. Steven was able to meet Roy Disney, Michael Eisner (CEO), and Frank Wells (CFO/COO), along with hundreds of other highly successful Disney

Cast Members (the term Disney uses for all employees) from all over the world.

While working as a front desk host at one of the Disney resorts, Steven had "got five minutes?" conversations with celebrities who were staying on the property as part of the "Star-a-Day" program. His fellow Cast Members were always perplexed at how Steven could start up a conversation with people like George Hamilton, Tim Allen, Ed McMahon, Steven Bochco (*Hill Street Blues* creator), Tom Cruise, Elisabeth Shue, Joey Lawrence, Kevin Costner, Jerry Bruckheimer, Nicole Kidman, and Barry Levinson—they would just keep talking to him for fifteen to twenty minutes when Steven had only asked that one "five minute" question. During the business seminars that were required as part of the program, Steven's fellow interns would grill him for stories from each of his "adventures," and apparently this knack for connecting with people made an impact, because at the end of his Disney College Program, out of 2,800 other program participants, Steven was voted "Most Likely to Be the Future President of Disney."

After he graduated from college, Steven was immediately offered a position at the Grand Floridian Beach Resort at Walt Disney World, Orlando. George Kalogridis, the general manager of the Grand Floridian, proved to be one of the finest leaders Steven ever had the pleasure to work with at Disney. George is now the president of Disneyland after an illustrious career spanning Florida, France, and now California. Steven made a positive impression, worked with some incredible leaders, and was promoted several times working in hospitality, costuming, laundry, casting, and Disney University. He was one of the first two salaried managers to teach *Traditions*, Disney's three-day orientation program for all new Disney Cast Members. This was a great honor, because up until that time, the Disney *Traditions* program was only taught by frontline hourly Cast Members.

Steven thought he would spend his entire career with Disney. The fascinating secret to his many different positions and promotions over several years was yet again "got five minutes?" Steven never knew it at the time, but it turned out that every promotion and career opportunity provided to him was brought by people he had interviewed using his "got five minutes?" strategy during his Disney College Program years. While this makes sense on the surface, the extraordinary point is that you must realize that some of these opportunities came five, six, or even seven years after the "got five minutes?" conversations! Now that's what I would call a memorable conversation.

Looking back on his Disney career, Steven was most proud to have worked with fellow Cast Members at Disney from eleven countries who spoke eight different languages, encouraging and coaching them to learn English so they would have more career opportunities within the Walt Disney Company. Amazingly, fifty-eight of these Cast Members have now been promoted multiple levels within the company, including into management positions. I asked why he got such a kick out of accomplishing that goal. He said, "Well, I have always had a big heart for the underdog, and I have always hated injustice and have always been drawn to help someone who is suffering or someone who has just given up on life. These are the kind of people that I love to help."

Eventually the entrepreneurial bug bit him again after working several years at Disney and completing his master's degree in organizational effectiveness. After leaving Disney and working with an entrepreneurial start-up company for several years, Steven decided to strike out on his own and start his own organizational change consulting company, Reconnect LLC. In his own classic style, he did not start the company with his own money, but with money from an angel investor. He built a thriving business, working with many organizations on service excellence, leadership effectiveness, and culture change. He has had this successful business for more than ten years.

Now he has decided to rebrand himself and change his business model. He currently helps other entrepreneurs build their dream businesses in record time. "It's my passion," says Steven. He loves the idea of being able to share his tools, tips, and techniques for helping entrepreneurs double their sales, triple their net profits, and retire in three to five years so they can take on new ventures or give back to causes they care about. The most humbling and rewarding aspect of his work is when Steven shares the mistakes he made along the way in the hopes that others can avoid the pain and heartache he endured over the years.

Steven says, "I have mastermind groups where people work together over a one year period, learning how to implement my strategies and learning from each other. I also provide private coaching for entrepreneurs who want to work with me one-on-one to help them achieve rapid breakthroughs in their businesses." He loves helping small business owners, particularly in the home services industry, build their businesses. Steven has developed an incredible system for developing instant credibility with prospective clients, while also achieving outstanding responses to his outrageous direct mail marketing techniques.

"I love seeing my clients succeed using my proven strategies and systems. I just love connecting with people and making a difference in their lives. It is the best feeling in the world, and besides I learn just as much from them as they learn from me," says Steven. He has been studying different methods of marketing for a dozen years and has become fascinated with marketing information products via the Internet. This is also very beneficial for his small business clients, because they might have intellectual property that would have a great deal of value being sold as an information product. "I am always attending seminars and conferences to learn about what's new in internet marketing, mobile marketing, information publishing, and social media, as I owe it to my clients. I'm keeping up with the latest developments in marketing and rapid growth for businesses," he says.

Apparently Steven has helped nine entrepreneurs retire in the past two years alone and has three more clients on track to retire within eighteen months. I am sure that every one of his mastermind group members and coaching clients are most grateful for connecting with Steven Rowell.

MO! Notes

1. **Make a connection.** Because Steven is fascinated with human nature and what makes each person unique, he is always trying to find a way to connect with each individual person. This results in people feeling appreciated and connected to him in a very sincere way.

2. **Have a big heart for the underdog.** Because Steven cares for people and does not tolerate injustice, he is often trying to help people who are underdogs. In a way, it makes so much sense that Steven coaches small business owners, the underdogs of the business world. It feels good to help people who need help, especially when they want help and are willing to use the help they receive.

3. **Teach what you need.** Steven pointed out to me that often the topics that he is teaching as a trainer and speaker are the topics that he needs the most himself and therefore ones he can learn from as well. We need to be aware of our own areas for development so that even if we are teaching something we can learn from it at the same time.

4. **Seek out mentors.** Even though Steven did not know why or how, he was fortunate enough in his life to have some significant mentors who helped him a great deal by both believing in him and providing resources. We need to seek out mentors and advisors who will give us the help and support that we need.

5. **Be a super learner.** Steven is always listening in to webinars, reading books and business magazines, and attending conferences. Being a super learner helps you stay motivated, fresh, and excited about what you're doing. Additionally, being a super learner will make you an amazing mentor and teacher for others.

6. **Be a constant giver.** Steven is always listening for what other people need and quickly offers up names, resources, suggestions, and ideas with no strings attached. Steven lives by the value of "give it away and it comes back to you many times over," knowing that it may not return for many years to come. He truly believes the gift is in the giving.

meMO!

- Decide that each time you speak to someone, you're going to say in your mind, *How can I serve or help this person?* After each meeting with someone, go back and review whether or not you took some sort of action to help him or her without any expectation of something in return.

- Don't limit your dreams. Write down all your big, crazy, gigantic dreams on a piece of paper and decide how you're going to make them happen. Remember that there are no rules; there's nothing stopping you except for yourself. Make the dreams big and you will win big.

- Decide on two to three people who can be of great assistance to you in the next year. Contact them by phone or e-mail, ask if they would be willing to be your mentors, and set up the first meeting to determine how your mentors can help you and what the mentoring process will look like.

- Think of a famous business person, find out if there is a book about them, and if there is, make a commitment to read it. It may be a book about Oprah Winfrey, Richard Branson, Mary Kay, Donald Trump, or Thomas Jefferson. It doesn't matter whether it is a business person from the present or the distant past. These books can be tremendously motivating and inspiring.

11

Elisabeth Nejmann: Flying High above the Crowds

Elisabeth was born in Vienna, Austria, on October 15, 1911. Her mother was a very proper woman with all the style and manners of a true Austrian lady. Her father was born in Poland and migrated to Austria because he did not want to fight for the Russians, who occupied Poland at that time. Her family was Catholic, but they eventually joined the Lutheran church.

Her father tuned musical instruments and later owned a circus. Yes, a real, live circus—every kid's dream! Elisabeth and her three brothers worked in the circus and traveled and performed all over Poland,

Romania, and Austria. It was a *big* circus with many
animals: elephants, tigers, alligators, and more. There
were acrobats, clowns, trapeze artists, bicycle riders on
high wires, and bareback horse riders. Elisabeth and her
brothers performed all these stunts to thrilling perfec-
tion. She would stand on her brothers' shoulders while
they were on the high wire and perform great feats, and
all without a net below! The audiences watched in awe
and loved it. Their circus was a great success and continued traveling for many years.

Elisabeth's father was very wise, however, and
knew that show business was not stable; he insisted that
each of his children also learn a trade to have a backup
plan in life. Her brothers learned cabinet-making and
other trades, and Elisabeth learned stenography and
business skills. Near the end of the war, she worked at a
newspaper. She remembers when all the news from the
paper had to go to Hitler's headquarters in Germany to
be censored before it could be printed.

World War II finally exploded. At the time, Elisabeth lived in Austria with her parents and her baby son,
whom she had out of wedlock. One night there was
an air raid, and Elisabeth's father yelled for everyone
to go to the underground shelter. They ran as fast as
the wind. Elisabeth's father was carrying her child, and
there was an earth shattering noise as a bomb hit them
both. Tragically, her child was killed instantly, and her
father died a few days later of his injuries. Many others
were also killed that day. War was ugly, and it didn't
discriminate in whom it touched. Elisabeth's family did
not want to bury her father and son in a mass grave, so
they wrapped up the bodies in a tarpaulin and buried

them nearby in a private area. No one should have to make such choices. Much later on, Elisabeth and her brothers went back to bury them both in a proper cemetery. The death of Elisabeth's father brought an end to the family circus forever.

Elisabeth's brothers did not want to join the army to fight for Germany, so two of them fled and lived mostly underground. Her oldest brother, however, stayed in Austria to take care of their grandmother.

Elisabeth became part of the underground, too. She learned how to negotiate for food, shelter, and safety. Food was severely rationed, so she would bake bread and barter it for meat. This is how they survived.

It had been many long and terrible years in Europe. Elisabeth, her three brothers, and their families had traveled and hid throughout much of the war. They had lived underground on relatives' farms. Finally the horror was over.

Because Elisabeth and her family had sponsors in America, they could leave Europe. However, they had to get to the American zone where the ships were. This was extremely dangerous with Germany occupying their country. Elisabeth and her brother's young family walked. They walked over mountains and through rugged terrain, sleeping in the woods and stopping at farmhouses for food and milk for the children. They walked and walked, and finally after three months they got to the American zone and to the ship. It was a triumph of human will.

Elisabeth really did not want to come to America, but her family carried on and said they would not go without her, so she reluctantly agreed to leave Europe, and so they all went to America.

Elisabeth Nejmann clearly remembers boarding the ship bound for America in Bremerhaven, Germany. World War II was still going on. She and one of her brothers, his wife, and two babies were going to the United States with money sewn into their coats.

Like many immigrants, they arrived in New York Harbor and settled into the lower east side of New York City. Elisabeth got a job on Fourteenth Street, working in a coffee shop of the famous Horn and Hardart chain. She went from job to job in New York City, each time getting a better one. She had to really study the street signs so she could get home at night, because she could not read English yet. But she eventually learned.

Elisabeth never married and never had more children. Today, she speaks with a heavy but understandable Austrian accent. She reads the newspapers, watches television, and knows what is going on in America better than most.

Elisabeth's brother and his family live in Long Island, New York, and they are all still very close. Her nieces affectionately call her "Tante" (Auntie). She has cousins living in Austria who come to visit her in the United States.

About fifteen years ago, she went back to Europe to see another of her remaining brothers before he died. Elisabeth recalls that nothing from her past is there anymore: not the houses, not the cemetery; nothing is the same. She says it didn't bother her, though; she had been through so much. She says, "Most people have no idea what war is like."

Elisabeth still lives independently. She exercises with weights twice a day to keep herself limber and in shape. She stands and sits as straight as a young girl. She cooks, cleans, does laundry, washes windows, hangs curtains, and shops every single day. She painted her apartment not too long ago. She is up at 5 a.m. and out of her apartment and on the 8 a.m. bus every day.

I know Elisabeth through my aunts Mary and Palma. Elisabeth lives across the hall from Mary, who is ninety-five years old. They look out for each other. They talk every single day, check on each other, and have a wonderful friendship. These are their golden years.

Her neighbors and friends describe Elisabeth as a very energetic woman. Every morning as she gets on the bus, she greets everyone with a very big, strong, happy "Good morning." When she gets off the bus back at her apartment, she gets kisses from each of the people waiting in line to board the next bus. They all love her; they cherish her and think she is "one of a kind." I would say they are right. Elisabeth Nejmann is "one of a kind," and still flying high above the crowds at one hundred years young.

MO! Notes

1. **Have a "plan B."** Have a backup plan in life; you never know when you might need it.

2. **Know that all things can be done.** If you can read, you can make it in another country.

3. **Be willing to do what is needed.** "You've gotta do what you've gotta do." Elisabeth survived because of her strong belief in survival and tenacity.

4. **Stop complaining.** Never, ever give up, and never complain about a gym workout. Elisabeth and her family walked for three months.

5. **Know that life is good.** (The t-shirt is right!) Life is better with a happy attitude and a great "Good morning."

6. **Be thankful for everything you have.** Be thankful daily if you have never witnessed war.

meMO!

- Focus on doing what you are good at. Have a backup plan. Make a list of your strengths and skills, and next to each put a job you might like to do that would make use of them. Refer to this list from time to time to refocus yourself or to propel yourself to the next move in your career.

- It is always a big plus to know another language. Decide that you will learn another language and *do it*. There are so many ways to do this today: online, through software, local community classes, community college evening classes, and more. If a foreign language does not interest you, learn a new computer skill. Once you have mastered that, go on to another, and another. The more diverse your skills are, the more desirable you will be in the job market. Doing this will also enrich *you*.

- When you find yourself complaining or feeling sorry for yourself, focus on others and what they might be going through or have gone through, and take the lessons from them. *Stop* yourself when you are feeling like having a pity party, and be thankful for what you have. Give thanks privately and publically. What you say to yourself and out loud to the world will change you for the better. It will also make you feel better about yourself.

- Each morning, have some serious "self-talk." Decide that you are going to leave your "not-so-positive self" at home. Decide what kind of person you want to show to the world that day. Be specific. For example, "I am going to have an upbeat, positive, powerful approach to others that I see, work with, and meet." Be very specific about how you will do this. See it in your mind and do it.

12

Bryan Dulaney:
Young Entrepreneur

I first heard of Bryan Dulaney when he was a college student. Mike, a friend of mine, called me and said, "Hey, I really think you need to meet with this guy named Bryan. He is motivated and really smart, and he wants to meet with you." I met Bryan at a local bookstore and was impressed by his ambition and his thirst for knowledge about the science of success. He was MOtivated!

Fast forward a few short years, and Bryan now owns his own business performing search engine optimization and creating Internet marketing strategies for several clients. Bryan and I had a chance to reconnect recently because I wanted him to work on a project for me. I was very impressed by how far he had come so quickly, and I wondered what creates that kind of drive and ambition in a young entrepreneur.

He grew up in the Chester County area of Pennsylvania about forty miles west of Philadelphia. He was born in Downingtown, and not long after, his family moved to the charming town of Honey Brook. (Who would not want to live in a place called Honey Brook?) There, he attended Honey Brook Elementary School and grew up with his parents and two younger siblings.

His initial exposure to the world of business was through his family. Several members of his family had an entrepreneurial spirit. Bryan's grandfather invented the fishing mini bucket, a very creative and inventive idea used by fishermen around the country. Being a talented inventor does not necessarily make a great business-minded person, however. After his grandfather invented the product and it gained popularity, his grandfather's partner in the venture took the idea, got it patented, and cut his grandfather out of the business. "I learned a lot from that," says Bryan. "I learned how businesses should be run and how you can have a great idea, but if the deal is not structured properly, it doesn't matter."

Bryan's father owned a company that ran trade shows relating to warehouse management technology and logistics. He and Bryan's uncle founded the company in the early '80s when the personal computer came on the market. Being interested in the world of business, Bryan worked for his father every summer, trying to figure out the secrets of their success. His first main motivator was his desire to duplicate his father's success by studying his business practices. He would spend hours on end talking to his father about these concepts.

At thirteen years old, Bryan decided that he would like to start a trade show in an industry he was interested in. At the time, his passions were surfing, skateboarding, and snowboarding.

Bryan did something I have never heard of any other thirteen-year-old doing: he interviewed his father to determine his keys to success in doing trade shows. His father explained the idea of market research: understanding the market before you approached it.

Bryan and his father bought every surfing, snowboarding, and skateboarding magazine known to man, as Bryan jokingly relates, and their office was filled with hundreds of magazines. Bryan would sit for hours at a time studying the manufacturers, vendors, and suppliers who might be best to approach about trade shows for that industry. He called companies to ask them for additional information and built a database to track the answers. As time went on, his passion for surfing, snowboarding, and skateboarding faded, but not his passion to be a business owner. The experience was very fruitful in helping him learn much about the principles of business and business marketing.

In high school, Bryan was very active in athletics, he participated in karate, and played on the baseball team. He believes this is probably one of the main reasons why his fledgling trade show initiative never happened. Being a superachiever, Bryan focused on karate and ended up becoming a second-degree black belt. He loved karate and feels like it helped him become more disciplined in both his actions and his thinking and helped him stay focused in school and in life.

Once Bryan graduated from high school, he was eager to get to college to start learning more and expanding his thinking. He enrolled at Slippery Rock University near Pittsburgh, Pennsylvania. Unfortunately, that university was known as a party school as opposed to a school known for academic study and serious intent by the students.

The first year he concentrated on academics and did well. Bryan decided in his second year, however, to get more involved on a social basis. He joined the most athletic and macho fraternity because of his background in sports. This eventually led to a great turning point in his life. It was a life-changing moment that, as he looks back, was a huge blessing, even though it almost caused his death (more on this a little later in this chapter).

He realized that what he was taught growing up was not the way he was living: "I was raised a Catholic and later on became a Christian and realized I had a massive disconnect between what I believed and how I was acting." He decided that his best approach was to leave Slippery Rock and enroll in a university that was more aligned with his values and beliefs.

Bryan did a great deal of research and finally settled on Clearwater Christian College, a small Christian college in Clearwater, Florida. It was a small school, very religious, and extremely conservative. Bryan had gone from a party school to an extremely religious school, and it was a big adjustment. The pendulum had swung in the other direction. The administration was very hard-core and the rules were strict. There was a curfew at 10 p.m. on weeknights and a strict dress code on and off campus. Even though this college was more aligned with his values, Bryan actually found it was too strict and restrictive, and he did not feel like he fit in. He left after one semester.

Even though Bryan didn't enjoy attending Clearwater Christian College, he was glad he had for that one semester because he met a remarkable classmate named JD who introduced him to another concept of personal development and lifelong learning. He encouraged Bryan to read *The 7 Habits of Highly Effective People*.

According to Bryan, "This book challenged me to become an avid learner of knowledge to further my ambition to become a business owner." He felt as if he had discovered a whole new world of knowledge and wisdom, and it opened up his eyes and his mind to the possibilities of success. The fire in him was lit, and he became a nonstop learning machine who fell in love with the works of many great motivational authors, including Anthony Robbins, Napoleon Hill, Wayne Dyer, and Joe Vitali. This also created in him a passion for Internet marketing and how information products were sold.

Bryan had friends who were attending Liberty University in Lynchburg, Virginia. Many of them told Bryan that he would love the university, so he looked into it and discovered a match for his principles and values and transferred there. At Liberty University, he finally found a happy medium: not a party school, but also not a school that was incredibly strict. He majored in business marketing with a minor in religion.

Every summer, Bryan would come back home to take time off from his studies. Bryan's grandmother was going to a gym in the area called The Synergy Club and said that Bryan *had* to meet the owner of the club, a gentleman by the name of Mike, who became a life-long friend. Bryan met Mike and they really hit it off. Mike had energy and vision and ran several success-ful businesses. He became Bryan's mentor. Bryan also helped Mike with marketing for his businesses, and to-gether they worked on a new product called "True U Discovery," a program designed to help young people discover their purpose and passion in life.

While still in his senior year at Liberty University, Bryan read Hypnotic Marketing by Joe Vitali and be-came fascinated with the idea of Internet marketing. He thought, *I can make money on the Internet from my dorm room? How cool is this?* He began experiment-ing with different Internet products and started reading books by gurus in the Internet marketing space, partic-ularly books by Yanik Silver. Bryan also learned about a free product called the "30 Day Marketing Chal-lenge" by Ed Young and decided to sign up and watch the video lessons daily, to see how it would go.

He built a website that was primitive by today's standards, put it out on the Internet, and made $750 in less than seven days. He was amazed by this experience, and it fueled his passion to begin a business in Internet marketing. Looking back on it, he chuckles, saying, "It wasn't even one of my products; I was an affiliate for someone else's product."

Bryan graduated from Liberty University and continued doing affiliate marketing while he was finishing up his MBA online. Once he finished his master's degree, he launched his full-time business, and within the first month he landed his first client, whom he was billing more than $8,000 per month. Now Bryan has a successful business helping clients with search engine optimization, Internet marketing strategies, and how to be more effective online in general.

Yes, I was so impressed with Bryan that he is now doing work for me on some search engine optimization strategies. He also has many information products under development that will soon be sold and marketed online and across the world. With an inventor as a grandfather and an entrepreneur as a father, I guess the apple did not fall very far from the tree.

I asked Bryan why he was so driven at such a young age. "I believe it was because I was exposed to my father and grandfather's entrepreneurial spirit, and I was fascinated by it. I have a vision of what I want to achieve in my career and in my life, and I am not going to limit myself to thinking small. Far too many people are not open to what is possible, and anything is possible, if you only believe and do the hard work to learn and take educated and researched risks in business."

He wants to become a monthly multimillionaire marketer with the goal of one million dollars per month in recurring residual revenue. I have no doubt that it will happen. He has a plan, he has a strategy, and he has the passion. He has MOmentum: "I travel when I want, where I want, and how I want, and I live a lifestyle where I have freedom of choice and where money is a nonissue."

By the way, Bryan Dulaney is only twenty-seven years old. He's a serial entrepreneur, second-degree black belt, and developer of many new information products; I can't wait to see what Bryan will do next, but I know this—someday I will see him on the cover of one of the business magazines as one of America's youngest multimillionaires.

MO! Notes

1. **Be persistent.** Bryan kept trying different schools until he found the right one. Sometimes you have to stick with it.

2. **Set your sights high.** You can't hit a target if you don't have one. And if you are going to have a target, why would it be small?

3. **Be a learner.** Learn from mentors like Bryan did, read great books of the ages, and study from masters in their craft. Be on a never-ending search for knowledge.

4. **Stop being swayed by age.** Bryan was looking to start businesses when he was thirteen. "Too young" and "too old" are just societal labels we can accept or reject. The limitation is all in your head.

5. **Try something.** Bryan believed an information marketing product would work from his dorm room. It did. It was worth trying—it launched his business! Too many people give up before they try.

meMO!

- What is one thing you have always wanted to do but have never tried? I'm sure you have heard this before, but life is very short. So what are you waiting for? Write it down on a piece of paper and answer the following question: Why haven't you tried it—what has stopped you? Answer that question and take action this week.

- If you often think of your age as being a barrier, think about why that is. Is your being too young or too old actually a legitimate reason not to achieve your dreams? Give this some thought this week and determine how you can overcome this form of negative thinking.

- If you're going to make significant progress in your life, both personally and professionally, you need to surround yourself with people who will help you do that. Make a short list of people you know who are motivating and stimulating and will help you get to the next level. Figure out a way to spend more time with those people, personally or professionally. Make it happen.

CHAPTER

13

Jennifer Thompson: The Harpist Who Went to Law School

When I first met Jennifer Thompson, she was the director of training for an organization, and the first thing that struck me about her was her sense of humor and her high level of energy. She just had a spark. Of course, it wasn't until much later that I realized that there was much more to her story. She had MO!

Jennifer grew up in a typical middle-class home in New Jersey. Her father was an account executive, and her mother stayed at home to take care of Jennifer and her younger brother. It was the classic television sitcom family—think *Ozzie and Harriet* or *My Three Sons*— just a nice, wholesome family of four.

At the age of nine, Jennifer attended a school recital and immediately knew she would like to be involved in music in a very serious way. When asked why, she says she has no idea why this feeling overcame her, but it did. A few days later, she announced to her parents that she wanted to play the harp. She remembers being at a piano and harp studio in New Jersey around that age and being able to pluck her first harp string, and she was in love. Her parents, who were not wealthy by any stretch of the imagination, gently explained that it was not possible. After all, even a smaller-sized harp could cost more than three thousand dollars. Not to mention a concert-sized harp could easily be triple that cost or more. This was not a deterrent to Jennifer, however, and she knew one day she would play the harp.

Jennifer came from a religious family, and after church on Sundays she went with her father to nursing homes where her father preached. She would always sit and listen to his sermons and then spend time visiting with the residents of the nursing home. Even though she was a child, she really enjoyed visiting with the residents, and many of them became longtime friends of both her and her family. She still has fond memories of many of the residents she got to know. One lady that they met named Gladys really impressed both Jennifer and her father on a continual basis because when she sat down and played the piano with one hand, she made it sound as if she was playing with both. As it turns out, Gladys had a disability and had been paralyzed at a young age, and she only had the use of one hand.

Jennifer continued her tireless campaign to somehow find a way to play the harp. When Jennifer was ten, her father was speaking with Gladys, and asked, "Do you know of any old harps or 'cheap' harps that I could get and fix for Jennifer? She really wants to play." Gladys turned to him, smiled, and said, "Well, why don't you just take mine?" As it turns out, Gladys used to play the harp, and her harp was in storage in upstate New York. Of course, Jennifer and her father made sure that Gladys was serious about giving Jennifer her harp. In the end, Gladys won the argument and Jennifer's dream came true. The next question that Jennifer's father posed to Gladys was, "I need someone to teach Jennifer how to play the harp—do you know anyone that could teach her?" Gladys said, "I'll teach her." So with the two big questions answered for Jennifer's future in harp music, the family made their way to upstate New York, where Jennifer's father spent five hundred dollars to get the harp out of storage.

Now Jennifer's family had a semigrand gold harp sitting in their living room. Yes, all things are possible. This was an amazingly generous gift. (Note that Jennifer had been praying for a harp for three years straight.) Now there was only one problem: the harp had been in storage for so long that the strings were ruined. So the lovely harp sat silent for an additional six months until the family had enough money for a new set of strings. Then Gladys taught Jennifer her first harp lesson, which lasted for half an hour, and it was only the overture for many lessons over the next six years until Jennifer was eighteen years old.

At the age of twelve, on her way home from school with her mother, Jennifer announced, "I am going to play the harp, and I am going to have a degree in law." Her mother rolled her eyes at her starry-eyed dreamer and said, "Just get through the seventh grade and college first!" But when Jennifer set her sights on something, she was determined.

The first step that she needed to take to pursue her dreams was to get a degree in music with an emphasis on the harp. In order to be accepted into the school of music of her choice, she had to audition. But because she had taken harp lessons on a private basis, she did not know what her skill level was. After her audition, her future harp instructor told her, "You are at the advanced level, and not only are we accepting you into the school, but we will also be able to get you scholarship money." It was a dream come true.

As they say, however, sometimes the dream does not match with the reality. For a year and a half, Jennifer was in conflict between the method she learned from Gladys and the method supported by her new instructor. After practicing five to six hours a day and enduring much frustration and stress, Jennifer decided to transfer from her current music school to one that was closer to home where she would be able to study with another prominent harpist who was more in line with her method of study. Jennifer knew that the transfer would set her back and graduation would be later than she originally anticipated.

In order to make additional money, Jennifer started playing at weddings. She loved doing it and loved performing in front of audiences. At one particular wedding though, Jennifer was playing the harp as the guests were waiting for the ceremony to begin. Unfortunately, the bride was late, so the people who hired her for the wedding asked her to keep playing and asked her to play louder as the large room kept filling with more guests. Jennifer played for an extended period of time and at a tremendous volume, which created a great deal of stress and exertion on her hands. When she was done playing, her hands were injured, both of them with their veins pulsating and grotesquely engorged with blood. It was incredibly painful, and no one knew if she would ever play the harp again. She was fortunate to find two chiropractors who helped her, and after eight months she was able to recover from her injury and start playing the harp seriously again.

Around the same time, Jennifer's family moved to Pennsylvania. Because her college expenses had increased, she was forced to drop out of school and go to work full-time. She had already transferred once during her college career and delayed her graduation. Now she felt like she couldn't even graduate at all. It was a time of great frustration and depression, and the idea of law school was somewhat of a joke.

Since she did not know where she wanted to work, she got a job at a bank. One day at the bank, she was talking to someone about the fact that she played the harp, and a music professor from a local university walked into the bank lobby and said, "Did I hear someone mention that you play the harp?" Jennifer, of course, volunteered that she was the one who was the harpist. "Well," he said, "I am a professor of music at the university, and we are looking for more music students and we would love for you to audition." The music department of the university awarded her a music scholarship, and Jennifer also got a job on campus to generate extra cash.

Finally, after six years of scraping, working, and going to school full-time, she was able to complete her four year music degree and graduated in 2001. For a few years, she wandered from job to job, working at a school, a grocery store, and a bank. She was still trying to figure out how law school was going to fit into her life—how she could somehow make it happen. On a whim, she filled out an application for a private law school in Pennsylvania, took her LSATs, and was instantly accepted and able to get student loans. She started the fall semester, fulfilling her dream of studying law.

She will always remember her birthday, because that is the day that she graduated from both undergraduate and law school. After studying and sitting for the bar, she landed a job teaching law at a local community college. Everything was finally starting to look up.

One weekend, she went to the shore and fell asleep in the sand while lying on the beach. When she woke up, she was extremely tired, more tired than normal, with an enormous sense of fatigue. Over the next several weeks and months, she started to lose her hair, and frighteningly, she exhibited many of the same symptoms as her good friend, Margo, who was suffering from Lymphoma. Jennifer went to see her family doctor, who did not discover anything abnormal and did not see a need to refer her to a specialist. She went to a doctor in New Jersey, and that doctor suspected that she might have thyroid issues, so he sent her to a specialist who ordered a needle biopsy of her neck. The results were negative, and Jennifer was told by the specialist that she was fine. Jennifer continued to feel sick, tired, and listless, however, so she knew something was wrong and she knew it was serious. She just could not get anyone to believe her. Finally, she made a persistent series of calls to her insurance company and they referred her to one of the best endocrinologists in the area. When he pulled out her charts and looked at the x-rays of her thyroid, he said, "See the grainy appearance on this x-ray? I don't like how that looks." He immediately ordered another set of biopsies.

One Sunday afternoon, her endocrinologist called: "Jennifer, I wanted to give you a call. We found cancer." Jennifer's surgery was scheduled for April of 2007. Sadly and ironically, she attended her friend Margo's funeral two weeks before her surgery.

As they were preparing Jennifer for her surgery, the entire family was praying, and she was very worried about the cancer spreading to her lymph nodes and her larynx. She knew that sometimes when people had their thyroid removed, they lost their voice. Her surgery went well though, and they caught the cancer soon enough to prevent it from spreading to other parts of her body. Her thyroid was removed successfully, but when she woke from her surgery she had no voice. She was terrified she would never be able to speak again. After waiting and praying for over a month after her surgery, she woke up on her birthday and her voice was back. She then went through a fifteen-month period of treatment and recovery, during which she was out of work. She had to move back in with her parents, and creditors were calling daily to collect overdue bills. She was also notified that she did not pass the bar exam. So then she sat around wondering what she was going to do with the rest of her life.

Sitting at home one day, she logged onto the Internet, and for some reason still unknown to her, she went to a Pennsylvania company website and looked at the employment section. She read about a training-and-development manager position, and she realized she was the perfect fit. Because Jennifer's father knew the CEO, he was able to put in a good word for her, and after several interviews, Jennifer was offered the job and discovered a new career in training and development. She learned a great deal in her position and then decided to move to another organization to head up business training and development there.

What's next? At this point, Jennifer is building her business of teaching harp and playing at special events and weddings while at the same time continuing to learn and develop her other skills while she figures out what she wants to do long-term. As she says so eloquently, "I know I have a purpose, and the Lord gave me specific talents and abilities and my purpose is not to squander them. I probably love life more because of some of the adversity that I have faced—so I am very careful and attentive in planning out the best life possible."

I don't think Jennifer Thompson ever squanders one minute of her life, no matter what she does, and I am sure with her level of persistence and tenacity she will be successful in anything that she chooses.

MO! Notes

1. **Be determined.** Many people, if faced with difficulties in their finances, career, and health, would likely give up at some point. Giving up is not part of Jennifer's makeup, however. Her faith motivates and inspires her and keeps her going.

2. **Have a purpose.** Jennifer is very driven to discover her ultimate purpose as a citizen of planet Earth. Is her purpose to be a harpist, a lawyer, or a learning-and-development professional? Who knows, but the point is that she's always *looking* for it—and people who are always looking for it will eventually find it or figure out how all the things in their lives can blend together into an ultimately purposeful plan.

3. **Love life.** Some people have never stared down the specter of cancer; some people have never sat and thought about what it would be like to die. Some people have never lost their best friend to this evil disease. Even if you have been lucky and not experienced such a fear or such a loss, is it is important to love life and to live life to its fullest, not taking one moment for granted.

4. **Be careful and attentive.** Many people go through life with a lack of direction, goals,

and strategy. Jennifer is always paying careful attention to what she wants to do next and how she's going to do it. This level of awareness and attention is a great tool for building success in your life.

5. **Ask for what you want.** Many people go through life never asking for what they want and never asking for resources or support, and as a consequence, they don't get it. However, if you ask for what you want and search for resources, it's amazing what you can find and what will be provided for you. All for one simple reason: you asked!

meMO!

- Do you know what you want for your life? Put another way, do you understand your life's purpose? If you do not understand your life's purpose, take the next sixty days and really make a concerted effort to define what you want your life to be about. To know what you're doing and why you're doing it can make a huge difference in your level of motivation.

- Are you putting in maximum effort? If you are not putting in 150 percent effort or you are doing things kind of halfway, then you need to determine why. Make a list of the things you're only putting minimal effort into. Get with a trusted advisor. Sit down and talk to them about it and ask them for ideas on how to increase your level of effort or your understanding of why your effort is not at the top.

- Make a list of things you want, and then determine who you need to ask for assistance in getting them. You see in many cases that the reason people have the things they want is because they had the boldness to ask for them. (And those who do not ask do not receive.) We are not saying that you don't have to do the work; we're saying that many times people just don't ask. When you ask for it, sometimes you get it.

14

Nick Rodrigues: Driving America

Nick Rodrigues was born and raised in Cuba. His father was a farmer with a lot of land. When Fidel Castro came to power and things got very bad for the people of Cuba, Nick's father wanted to escape with his family and come to America.

The Castro regime found out about this and deemed Nick's father and one of Nick's brothers enemies of the state and put them in jail. His brother stayed in jail for three years and his father for ten long years.

Nick went to school in Cuba until the sixth grade. Then he had to go to work in construction, doing hard labor, to make money and help his family survive while his father and brother were imprisoned.

MO!

In 1980, six years after Nick's father was released from prison, Castro opened the gates and allowed all political prisoners (plus many others in prison) and anyone else to leave Cuba. When he was just sixteen years old, Nick—along with his mother, father, oldest brother, and his oldest brother's wife and three children—came to America.

You may remember the Mariel boatlift, which was a mass exodus of Cubans who departed from Cuba's Mariel Harbor for the United States between April 15 and October 31, 1980. This was brought on by a sharp downturn in the Cuban economy that led to internal tensions and a bid by nearly ten thousand Cubans to gain asylum at the Peruvian embassy. Because of this, the Cuban government announced that anyone who wanted to leave could do so, and the exodus by boat began. Cuban Americans organized it with the agreement of Fidel Castro. As many as 125,000 Cubans made it to the shores of South Florida.

Nick and his family were among them. They traveled on a forty-eight-foot boat with fifty passengers for sixteen hours in extremely rough seas. To this day, Nick remembers it well. They finally hit America, landing in Key West.

The US government and the Red Cross had set up a station where the boats were landing. As people arrived, they were helped off the ships and given blankets, hot food, and water and soap for showers. They were also given shelter and beds to sleep in for the night.

Early the next morning at eight o'clock, buses transported the Cuban arrivals to the Key West Airport, where they boarded a plane bound for Sparta, Wisconsin. When they landed in Sparta, school buses awaited them, and they were driven forty-five minutes to Fort McCoy, an active Army installation.

At Fort McCoy, the Cuban refugees were housed in Army barracks and cared for while the immigration process took place. Nick and his family were there for one month. During the immigration process they tried to contact family members living in the United States that would vouch for each Cuban and agree to house them and help them start their new life in America.

Nick's family had a cousin living in New Jersey. Once Immigration Services confirmed this and the cousin agreed to sponsor them, they were put on a plane bound for New Jersey. Nick and his family lived with his cousin for one month.

Within that month, Nick, his father, and his brother found jobs and found two apartments to house their two families. They were on their way to life in America. Their dream was coming true!

Nick and his father worked at a dairy plant. Nick worked the milk-packing machine and continued to work there for six years. After three years, they had saved up enough money to buy a house where Nick and his parents could live.

Nick found a new job with a local limo company using his own car and did this for six more years. During those six years, he saved enough money to eventually go out on his own and start his own limo business.

At first, it was just Nick and his car, and then he acquired a stretch limo, and then another town car and soon another. Nick has now run his own limo business for fourteen years.

Seventeen years after Nick left Cuba on that infamous Mariel flotilla, he went back to visit his remaining family there. While he was there, he met a woman by the name of Damarys. During subsequent trips back to Cuba, they fell in love and were finally married in Cuba. Nick came back to the United States without her to try to get the papers processed for her to move to America to live with him. Damarys was also pregnant with their child.

With his family's support and the help of professionals, it took Nick four long years to get the documents approved to allow his wife and their young daughter to move to the United States.

Today, they live in New Jersey, happy to be in America, working hard and raising their now twelve-year-old daughter together. Nick's eighty-three-year-old mother also lives with them, and his oldest brother lives with his family in Tampa, Florida. Nick also has an older daughter and a son, from a previous marriage, who live in the United States. Nick's father passed away in 2007 at the age of eighty-seven.

As for Nick's limo company, it is doing just great. You can often see him at the bottom of the escalator near the baggage claim in any of the three New York City area airports, awaiting a passenger. He often wears his beret to help identify him. He looks pretty smashing in it!

I asked Nick about what motivates him, and he said, "I want to always do my best, improve myself. I don't want to stay in the same place; I want to get ahead. I like to work, I like to work hard, and I am happy to." Doesn't this sound similar to many of our ancestors who came to America since 1776? As Warren Buffet once said during an interview with Charlie Rose, "I was born lucky, I was born in America."

Nick told me that he owes it all to his father's wish for a better life for his family. Nick says, "My father felt *really* American." And he was.

MO! Notes

1. **Be willing to be brave.** Be brave enough to speak up for your human rights.

2. **Have a dream.** Nick's father dreamt of a better life for his family. Nick had the same dream for his family. Focusing on that dream and working toward their goals helped Nick and his father attain it.

3. **Ask for help when you need it.** There are always many people who are willing to help others. Take the help when you need it, and remember to pay it back someday too.

4. **Go back to your roots.** Sometimes you need to go back to your roots to find the right person to complete you. In Nick's case, it took a trip back to Cuba after seventeen years to find the love of his life.

5. **Hold onto love.** Love is, and always will be, undefeated. Nick never gave up though it took him four long years to bring his wife and daughter to America.

6. **Have style.** Wearing something that gives you a signature style, like Nick's beret, can make people remember you and also identify you in a crowd.

7. **Work on you.** If you don't want to stay in the same place, try to improve yourself, and start by doing your best.

8. **Embrace change—don't fight it.** Embracing change and being proud of the country you live in can feel really great!

meMO!

- Right now, write down three short-term goals to be accomplished this week. Write down three midterm goals to be accomplished this month and three long-term goals to be accomplished this year. Look at this list every day, and work on one item at a time, focusing on each until it is accomplished. Then add another goal to the list and keep going. This is how goals are attained and things get done.

- If there is someone in your life that can help you with something you wish to accomplish, ask for his or her help today. Asking others to help you will *help you*, and remember to always repay them in some small way and to help others along the way too.

- Always dress in your own style and be true to this style. People may remember you better by a style that is uniquely yours. If you need to find a style to call your own, there are style experts in most retail stores that can help you. Go to your favorite store and ask.

- Be true to your beliefs and opinions, regardless of who is listening. You will earn the respect of others by being true to yourself. Remember, however, to also be respectful and discreet.

15

Hans Trenker: Lemonade Man and Much More

When you looked at Hans Trenker, he was lively and full of spirit, and it would shock you to know that he had a tough life full of many trying times.

Hans was born in Germany. When he became a teen, he was quickly taken from his family and put in the Hitler Youth against his will. He was against the war and fled to the United States on a slow boat and wound up in Chicago. Once in Chicago, he did all the odd jobs he could to stay alive and make a living.

One day he met a young girl and was smitten with her. Shortly after, they married and had two children: a girl and a boy. Life seemed complete.

Several years later, Hans came home from work and his wife told him that she wanted a divorce because she had fallen in love with the mailman. *Really*, the mailman! (I know, it sounds like the plot of some soap opera.)

After many months of trying to make his marriage work and after many discussions, Hans saw no way to change his wife's mind. She was in love with the other man. It was the most difficult decision Hans ever had to make, but he decided to leave Chicago, leave his children, and go far away. He ended up in Florida. His ex-wife moved with the children and never told him where they were going. He tried desperately to find them for many years, but he never heard from his ex-wife again. He had lost his family.

After a few years in Florida, Hans met Julie. She was the love of his life. They married and had a wonderful life working and playing together and sailing around the Florida Keys on a boat that Hans saved up to buy. They were a very active, energetic couple, both with spirits that embraced life.

Julie was a nurse and Hans was an entrepreneur in the garment production business. Hans traveled a great deal, and on any given Friday night, if you happened to be at the Atlanta airport, you might have caught him boarding his flight home after a long week on the road. This is where I met Hans, and we became airport friends. I met Julie shortly after, and my husband and I enjoyed a wonderful friendship with them for many years.

One of the best memories for us was our sailing trip with Hans and Julie—particularly the vigor and the love of life and the sea that Hans had. He also made the very best lemonade on Earth. It was always the perfect drink after a hot day on the boat. Hans often rejoiced in the simple, delicious flavor of it as he savored every icy drop. There is joy in simplicity, and sometimes in simplicity there is joy.

We often marveled at how Hans rejoiced in the many simple things in life. I learned a lot from him about it. He lived his life this way 24/7.

Then one day ten years later, we received an invitation from Hans to come to his home for a party. He said that he wanted us to meet his two children and their families. *We never knew he had kids!* Hans had never told us of his early life in Germany or Chicago, and it was a very big surprise. We, of course, went to the party to meet Hans's kids, in-laws, and a few of his grandchildren. They were all wonderful. A few days after the party, Hans told us his story of fleeing Germany, going to Chicago, and then leaving there to come to Florida.

Shortly after Hans left Chicago, his ex-wife told the children he had died. She then married the mailman and had more children. They were all raised as one family.

Fifteen years or so later, Hans's ex-wife came home one day to tell her mailman husband she wanted a divorce because she was in love with yet another man. The mailman was enraged and killed her and then himself. It was a terribly tragic time for the children. Hans's daughter and son, as young adults, began raising the younger children on their own.

One day, Hans's daughter found in her mother's address book the name and address of Hans's cousin in Germany. She decided to write to her to tell her about all that had happened.

Hans's cousin forwarded the letter on to Hans, and it became apparent to him that his children thought he was dead. Now he finally knew where they were! It was a miracle. Hans immediately got in touch with his children, and then came their visit to Florida and the party.

Hans, Julie, and the entire family were thrilled to be reunited, and it was the happiest time for them all. It was so great for my husband and me to share it with them.

The week after the family visit, Hans was painting his roof and did not feel well. Julie, being a nurse and also knowing how healthy Hans was, insisted he be checked. After many tests, the doctors told Hans he had very late-stage, aggressive stomach cancer. Five weeks later, Hans died.

I visited him just once in the hospital. He was reflecting on his life. He was studying the pattern on the wallpaper and telling me it had been hung incorrectly. He was discussing religion. He was talking about his mother and father. He was speaking in German. He was in-between here and there.

He asked that I not come back to see him. This still hurts today, but I know he was protecting me. He did not want me to be upset by what I might see in him. We said our good-byes, and I never saw him again. He wanted me to see him in the best light.

Julie, his children, and his grandchildren grieve for the loss of this very special, unique, dignified man. They have all learned so very much from him, especially his love of life and how to rejoice in the simple things. They now have each other, and Hans lives on *in* each of them and *with* all of them as a family. And on really, really hot days—yes, it's true—we all still miss his lemonade.

MO! Notes

1. **Rejoice in life.** Embrace life and enjoy the little things. Remember to smell each and every rose. Do the things you love, and remember why you love them. Rejoice in them!

2. **Give up when you have to.** Sometimes you have no choice but to give up the hunt. Human nature is to keep searching for what we have lost, but sometimes you have to give it up and hope it will find you again one day.

3. **Don't worry; be happy.** Be happy with what you have. Share what you have with others and the reasons you are happy. This may inspire others, and it will most certainly motivate you.

4. **Don't judge.** Never judge another. Until we have walked in another's shoes, we never really know what their life has been like and why they made the choices they have or do the things they do.

5. **Use a pro.** Get a professional to hang the wallpaper, and never underestimate the power of a really good lemonade.

meMO!

- Make it a point to stop at least once a day and take a break, be it a coffee break or a short walk. During that break, focus on your surroundings: the people, the flowers, and the pictures on the walls. Focus on something other than your job or your struggles. Focus on what is good around you. Take some deep breaths and relax, even if just for a few minutes. Taking breaks will help your spirit and your attitude.

- If you ever face an issue or problem that seems to be impossible to fix, leave it alone and come back to it in a week or so. Then take another look at the issue, and with fresh eyes you might find the solution. If not, leave it alone for another week. If you still can't find a solution, give it up. Often the wasted efforts far outweigh the problem. Think of which is more valuable: finding the solution or saving the time by giving it up and moving on to what else matters.

- Some things need a professional, like hanging wallpaper. If you are not an expert, decide if it is worth the time and effort to do it yourself. If not, spend the money for a really professional job.

CHAPTER

16

Joe Fleming:
Skycap with True Spirit

It is hard enough to have to be at work every morning at 4 a.m., but to *want* to arrive an hour early at 3 a.m. is downright unusual. It's not unusual for Joe Fleming, however. Joe arrives to work at 3 a.m. along with a few of the other guys so they can get their minds right. During this hour, Joe thinks about life, thinks about the day, relaxes, meditates, and just gets his mind ready for the day ahead. Joe told me he is very disciplined. He has never been late for his job, not one day, ever!

Joe Fleming is a skycap at the Fort Lauderdale airport in Florida. He works for a company called Bags Incorporated. Joe and his coworkers are responsible for checking in, tagging, and picking up the bags for

Delta Airlines curbside. Not an easy task at best, and then throw in the weather elements and the passenger personalities and you have a really challenging job. Joe does it all with professionalism, ease, eloquence, and a gentle "can do" manner. Let's be honest—this is a hard job that many people wouldn't really want. Once someone had the job, he or she wouldn't want to go to work early, but Joe does because he makes it so. He is MOtivated.

When you meet him for the first time, and he takes over checking you in and taking care of your luggage, you know he is special. You know your bags will get to where they need to go. This man cares!

I met Joe in 1972 when he had just moved to Fort Lauderdale from Atlanta and got the skycap position, at that time with Aircraft Services International. He was the very same on that first day as he is today. Joe Fleming is a genuine gentleman who does his job well with a caring "Spirit of God" attitude. It shows and it shines right through even at 4 a.m. *Really!*

Joe was born in Eastman, Georgia, and started school there. His mother raised him on her own; his father was not in his life. At ninety-six years old, Joe's mother is still an upbeat and happy person. Joe says that it was his mother who molded him. She made the difference.

In 1962, Joe moved to Florida to go to a trade school to learn how to be a computer repair technician. Having difficulty finding a job after school, Joe moved back to Atlanta in 1965 to accept a position as a warehouse manager. He worked there until 1972, when he moved back to Fort Lauderdale and got the skycap position. Joe worked two full-time jobs back then. While he worked as a skycap, he also worked for Modern Age Furniture in Miami. His job there was to make sure the right furniture got on the right truck going out for deliveries.

Joe married his wife Betty in 1975. They have been married for thirty-six years now and have four daughters and one son. Their oldest daughter, Selina, and youngest daughter, Monica, graduated from Florida A&M University in Tallahassee, Florida, and Monica is still attending graduate school there. Their second daughter, Monica, graduated from the University of Florida with a master's degree in education and is a teacher in Gainesville, Florida. Jennifer, their third daughter, works as a childcare professional in Palm Bay, Florida. Joe's son, Ralston, lives in Atlanta, Georgia, is a barber and an entrepreneur.

When I ask Joe's friends about him, they say he is a person of value. He doesn't just do, he *really* does, and he believes in what he does no matter what it is.

Joe says to me, "Being a black man is hard, but you can be a good citizen." Joe told me that his dear mother, his teachers, and his whole community raised him. He was taught to be "honest, be straight in what you do, don't cheat, no smoking, no drinking, and no cursing. Let people see 'The Spirit of God' in you."

As for Joe's children, he gives them true, genuine love and tries to set an example for them. He does charity work feeding the homeless and sits on the board of Human Resource Development, Inc., which helps first time homebuyers with the process of home-buying and more.

No matter the time of morning, the weather, airline delays, or the amount of baggage to be checked, Joe Fleming is always the same. He is always consistently pleasant and efficient. He told me that he loves people. In his job, he tries to be as kind, happy, and upbeat as possible to his flying public. He says, "When you deal with so many people every single day, you have to be kind, because you have no idea what they are going through, what they might have been through, and why they are flying. I try to let the Spirit of God in me be seen."

After interviewing Joe and reflecting on the many dozens of times that Joe met me at the curbside, I realized he has always called me by my name, always with a smile, and always ready to get the job done. I can hear it in my head: "Hello, how are you this morning and where are you going today?" And for the good-bye's, "Good-bye, have a great trip and see you next time. Give my best to your family." Now that really is the Spirit of God coming through. Thank you, Joe, and see you next flight.

MO! Notes

1. **Get up and be early.** It helps to get where you are going early to have time to get your mind ready for the task at hand.

2. **Do it right.** No matter what the job is, do it well and efficiently.

3. **Always listen to your mother.** Listen to your mother, know what you really love about her, and try to be like her.

4. **Have friends.** A true support system can be far reaching. It can include teachers as well as people in your local community.

5. **Lead the way.** Be an example to others and let your true goodness shine through. Others will notice and will be changed by this goodness even though they may not know what this goodness is called. Joe's goodness is "the Spirit of God."

6. **Serve others.** No matter how busy you are and how many hours you work, make time for others and be charitable. Teach others to do the same.

7. **Love the world.** Love is a gift we must give to one another.

meMO!

- Plan the time on your calendar to get to where you are going at least ten minutes early. If possible, make that twenty to thirty minutes. Planning this way allows you to reflect on the task at hand and be prepared for things that go wrong. Dependable people do this every single day.

- Reflect back on the people who influenced you the most as a young person. Pick three people and then write down three things about each of them that you would like to copy. For example, "Mother—great planner, Uncle—great communicator." Put these attributes into every task that you do. Write them down on your daily task list, and build them into every document you prepare and conversation you have.

- Ask others for their help. If you are struggling with an issue or are just stuck on something, make a list of people you can ask for help, opinions, and guidance. Be frank with them, and tell them exactly what you are doing and what you are asking of them. Take notes. Try each one of their tactics, and find at least one that works. If you find one, don't stop at this one—try all of them. There are often several ways to solve a problem.

- Make time every week for a person in need. Find someone that can use your help and help them. Block out this time on your calendar, weekly or *at least* monthly, and take the time to help this person. In turn, ask that person to do one small favor for you. Try it!

17

Pearl Deery:
Pearls of Wisdom

Have you ever seen the movie *The Flying Nun*? I watched it again recently, and it so reminded me of Pearl Deery. She is not only a remarkably unique person in her own right, but she also certainly fits her name. She is so very *dear* to this world in so many ways. She has so much energy and is so MOtivated and dynamic, you expect her to fly! She just has that kind of special quality.

Yes, Pearl is a nun. I know you are thinking of the stereotypical nun you would imagine wearing a habit and robes, but that is not Pearl. She is a true character and a true individual. Some might say she is a real "hoot!"

Pearl just turned sixty-one, and when she became a nun, things were much different. Pearl was attracted to the life of being a sister when she was eighteen years old. She had wonderful memories of her own education and liked to help people find their passions in life. Her family was very supportive and said, "Try it, Pearl; try being a nun, teach, and if you like it, you can stay with it." Pearl loved it and is still a nun today. She truly fell in love with her calling. How many people love what they do? How many people love their work? How many people feel their work is a calling? Not many people I meet. Isn't that kind of sad?

Pearl started in a convent in a small town in Ireland called Dundalk. The town is situated where the Castleton River flows into the Dundalk Bay and is equidistant between Belfast and Dublin. She was never allowed to leave the convent and couldn't even go to stay with her mother when her father passed away. It was the strict way of the convent back then, and she accepted it. Over the years, things have changed in the world of nuns, and now Pearl lives in a holy family parish with four other nuns, wears regular clothes (but usually not too stylish), drives a car, uses a computer to send e-mails, and has a life like most of us. Yes, nuns now have technology too.

Pearl is so very interesting to talk to about life because she has a simple, almost naïve perspective of the world. Her viewpoint is quite refreshing and most entertaining.

Pearl's main work in the sisterhood is education and nursing. For many years, Pearl has served teens through education and youth work events.

At the age of fifty, Pearl was asked to go and live in Nigeria for two years to work as a teacher in a tiny village in the middle of nowhere. Now imagine, she had never left Dundalk in her entire life, never been out in the world, never been on a plane, and she had agreed to move to Nigeria for *two* years! Now that is MOxie!

In Nigeria, Pearl was in constant fear of dying of some disease or a car accident. This never stopped her, however, and she never turned back. One night she was traveling down a dirt road with her Nigerian driver, whom she was quite fond of and who became a very important part of her life while she was in Nigeria. As they were driving along, they saw a dead body on the side of the road. The driver was afraid to stop for fear he would be accused of murder. Pearl, however, insisted that they do something and got the driver to go to the nearest police station to report what they had discovered. Pearl then led the police officer and the driver back to pick up the body. She said she couldn't tolerate the thought that this man wouldn't be buried with dignity, and so the man was. Perhaps the real reason Pearl was sent "with faith" to Nigeria was for this man. While her driver lacked courage, Pearl had conviction and put aside any worry about being accused.

Pearl survived the two years in Nigeria without injury, but when she arrived back home in Ireland, she was in a terrible car accident and broke her neck.

Fortunately, she fully recovered with no long-term impact, which is amazing in itself.

Pearl is the kindest, nicest, and most amazing lady in so many ways. She sees things with different eyes and loves and lives life to its fullest. Everything seems new to her. She has a great sense of humor too. Her friend Leo Sullivan asked her once what she was going to wear to a family wedding, and she replied, "I have two suits: a blue one for funerals, and a pink one for weddings." Her friend Leo replied, "I hope you will wear the pink one," and she did, with sandals! Pearl says, "Being a nun allows me to wear whatever is comfortable, because people will say, 'Oh, she's a nun; what does she know?'" This also shows her insight into human nature.

Today, Pearl is still a teacher in Ireland and a volunteer with the Apple Tree Foundation, where young people can go to get in touch with themselves and their individual gifts of creativity. Pearl has also helped to get much-needed funding for the Youth Café, where kids can go to experience music, dance, films, and exhibitions. For many of the kids, it is the first time they can experience any of the arts, live. Pearl says that kids love energy and honesty, especially kids who carry lots of pain, often from their own families. Pearl has a diverse variety of friends, including fellow nuns, others that were nuns but left the sisterhood, married couples, and colleagues. Her friends say that she is very much a "people person." She enriches her life by being busy with the community. She takes joy in living with people through their ups and downs and often can help them through it all.

Pearl is sometimes overworked, but as she says, "My body is my friend, and when it tells me to slow down, I do." How many of us listen to our own bodies' advice? Not many, I am sure. She also says that she could not be anything but what she is, because she believes we are who we are "inside out." She is a great believer that when we "work together," none of us is the greater or lesser, but we are all equally important to the greater good. Do you think Pearl's ideas could be useful in many places in the world? I have no doubt.

There is no better example of serving others than Pearl Deery. Sometimes we donate our time, our belongings, or our money to charities or people who need help. Pearl, on the other hand, has dedicated her entire *life* to serving others. She has devoted her work and her time to the greater good to help others and to enrich all our lives.

Pearl Deery is a rare pearl and the rarest of all the "human pearls" who bring beauty and light to the world.

MO! Notes

1. **Try it; you might love it.** Often we need a nudge from others who know us to try out a new career. Sometimes others see in us what we do not see in ourselves. Maybe we should trust the insight of others more often.

2. **When opportunity knocks, go for it.** Nothing ventured, nothing gained. Sometimes opportunity comes to us for what seems like one reason but ends up being for another totally unexpected reason.

3. **Laugh at yourself.** (Even if you are a nun!) Finding humor in yourself and the world will make others open up to you, talk to you more, and learn from you. *You* will also learn from them.

4. **You're never too old.** Age is only a number. You are never too old to try something new, move to a new place, or take on a new challenge. Your youth and vibrancy are determined by the people you hang out with, how you think, how you act, and how much you learn from others and your experiences.

5. **Follow your instincts and do what it right.** Like Pearl with the body on the side of the road, do what you know is morally right in every instance. You may have been put into a situation for reasons beyond your own understanding.

meMO!

• Remember to listen to what others say about what they see in you and how they view your talents. If others are not saying things about you, ask them what they see and get their read on *you.* Then, take their advice.

• Look and listen when opportunity knocks. Listen with your third ear (to what is being said and what is *really* meant by what is being said) for opportunities that come your way. These usually come for a reason. Seize the moment and remember to ask questions.

Within two days, take action on the opportunity. Follow up and follow through.

- Use this technique at least once a day. When things get busy or stressful, go to a memory, story, or joke in your mind that will make you laugh. If it is something that makes you laugh at yourself, even better. Humor is a great antidote to life's troubles.

- Make a list of the things you want to do and the places you want to go this year. Write down at least three goals, and then make a plan to do everything on your list within twelve months. Be very specific when making plans and setting goals. The more specific you are, the greater the chance you will accomplish these things.

18

Jesse Julian Cohen:
The Smile Guy

Have you ever met someone whom you know is an old spirit and will probably make a difference in every life he or she touches? (Don't deny it—I know you have.) Well, that is how Jesse Julian Cohen makes you feel when you come in contact with him. He is one of those MOtivated people!

At any given time you may find Jesse in a crowd at an airport, in a mall, or on a street corner, sporting his two-sided smile sign. You see a young guy wearing jeans, sneakers, and probably a backpack, looking relaxed, nonthreatening, and so very innocent. Jesse ambles along with a great big happy face sign, and when he makes eye contact with a passerby, he flips his sign over and it says, "SMILE!" You think to yourself, *Is this kid nuts? Is he mentally OK?* I mean, why would someone do this? What is even more amazing, however, is that it works! People's spirits are lifted, they smile, and they even change the way they walk!

I first came upon Jesse at an airport while I was going to my gate to catch a flight. Jesse was also catching a flight that day. Carrying his smile sign is what he was doing to spend his time before he boarded his plane. I was very curious about him. Who could resist talking to him to find out why he was doing this? I knew I couldn't. I had to find out the story behind the smile. He was a delight: easy to talk to, outgoing, mellow, and so totally into just wanting to make people feel better. I loved his spirit and his total belief in what he was doing. It was not naïveté; it was *real* and *total* belief!

Jesse has always been interested in world peace and understanding the balance between good and evil. The smile sign is his way to create a public memorial to "promote peace and love through *love*." Peace on Earth is his goal, and he is pursuing it with a cardboard sign. It sounds ridiculous, doesn't it?

He started doing this with a sign that had the peace symbol on it, and then a spontaneous thought came to him to put the word "smile" on the other side. He started sticking his sign out of windows wherever he went, from cars at traffic lights to airport gates and everywhere he went. He would just flip the peace symbol side over and it would say, "Smile." Today, Jesse's sign has a happy face on one side, and then he flips it over like a coin to the other side with the word "SMILE!"

A true hero to Jesse is Juan Mann, the Australian peace activist who founded the Free Hugs campaign. Julian read about him and was fascinated. Juan Mann walks around with a cardboard sign that says "free hugs," and then all you see is Juan hugging complete strangers, like in the famous video of Juan Mann. It reminded me of an author and speaker years ago by the name of Leo Buscaglia who after a talk hugged everyone in the audience. He would stay afterward and hug a thousand people. Maybe you have heard about Leo Buscaglia or have seen Juan Mann, and maybe it made *you* smile. Juan Mann is where Julian got the inspiration to do his "SMILE!" thing.

Jesse thinks the message he is giving is much stronger without being spoken. "*You* don't need words spoken to express a feeling," he says with tremendous passion in his voice. He also says that most people smile and laugh out loud, but he thinks that there are lots of people who don't smile enough because of life's difficulties. "People forget to smile," and his sign reminds them to. Jesse says that doing it makes him happy, and it makes him smile too. You could say he is a smile ambassador.

When you have a conversation with Jesse, it becomes apparent right away that he is a kind, gentle, and very selfless guy. He talks very fondly of his parents, brother, and grandparents. He has a heart for others. His love is contagious.

Jesse is an artist in every sense of the word. He plays guitar, writes poetry, acts in plays, writes short stories, and sings. He also does set design and construction, sculpts, paints, and does video production. He designed a mural for the theater lobby of a school he went to and has done countless other similar projects. *Wow!*

He attended the New World School of Arts in Miami, Florida, and was involved in the "Ring Master for the Arts," an event where students perform their expertise before an audience.

Jesse's grandparents on his father's side were artists. His grandfather was a sketch artist and his grandmother, Julia Cohen, has some of her work displayed at a few art museums in New York City.

I asked Jesse if he has ever had any negative people approach him or if anything strange has ever happened to him while sporting his sign, and he said, "I never got beat up! I have just always been outgoing." One of his friends told me that by knowing Jesse and watching him do his "SMILE!" thing she has been inspired to become more social and outgoing herself. Jesse's smile sign goes way beyond just making folks smile more.

Jesse and his smile sign drew me in. His beliefs, courage (it's not easy to stand in public with a sign and say nothing), and his peaceful "Just doing my small part to try to change the world" attitude surely not only made me smile but also uplifted me at that moment. Think about it: How many people would have the courage to do this? How many people would worry about being ridiculed or being made fun of? How many would be flat-out embarrassed? Jesse isn't.

Now, as Paul Harvey would say, "Here is the rest of the story." A small piece of information that I did not previously mention is that Jesse Julian Cohen is only sixteen years old. That's right: only sixteen.

If a small portion of our youth is anything like Jesse, we are in good and capable hands for having peace in the world. Thank you, Jesse, for making the world a better place and for reminding us to smile. It is something many of us forget to do.

MO! Notes

1. **Follow your heart and what you really believe in.** Even if others think what you are doing is simple, naïve, silly, or just a "kid thing," do what you believe can make yourself and others just a little bit happier. It just might work; have the courage to do it, and don't worry about what others think.

2. **Be creative and reinvent your original idea.** Once the beginning of an idea is born, keep it going, and keep it new, fresh, and strong by reinventing what you do and how you do it. The progression of an idea or skill will yield more results.

3. **Don't make age a factor.** We can all learn from someone else in the world, regardless of age or status in life. Don't discount someone because he or she is young.

4. **Have a hero to help you propel your ideas.** When you hear about someone doing something that moves you in some way, find out why and how he or she did it. Use that

knowledge to mold your idea or passion, and then make it your own. Find what you are passionate about, learn who else may have similar feelings, and use that as a springboard.

5. **Use the talents you were born with.** Not everyone is born with creative or artistic talent. If you were, use your talent to express yourself, share it with others, and expand it in a 360-degree way.

meMO!

- Don't be afraid to reinvent your original idea. The progression of an idea or skill will find more results. Write down the pros and cons of your idea and how it is being done. Next to each con, come up with a way that you can stay true to the idea while turning the con into a pro.

- Take a look at how young people are doing things today. Make a list of what you like, and then next to each item, write down how you can utilize this tactic in your job or your life.

- Find a mentor. It can be anyone from the past or someone living now. What do you like about what they did and who they are? Write these down. In a second column, next to each, make a correlation to it about what you want or need to accomplish. In a third column, write down how you will go about emulating your mentor. Now take one item a week and work on it until you have accomplished your goal, and then move on to the next. Keep going!

19

Mac Greentree:
Auctioneer Extraordinaire

Mac Greentree was a farm boy, born in 1944. He was the oldest of three boys and grew up in Kenton, Ohio. By all young boys' standards, it was a dream come true to live on a farm with cows and horses to play with. When he was fourteen, his family moved to Iowa, where they had a bigger farm with seventy dairy cows and more horses.

Then one day while they were playing with the horses, Mac got kicked in the right eye. The doctors tried to save his eye but could not. Mac has had a glass eye since then and has learned to live with his limited sight.

Today, Mac says he has worn out two glass eyes already but sees more than most other guys see! When you meet Mac, talk with him, and feel his spirit and love for people and life, you know he is right.

Mac started college and went for a year and a half to the University of Northern Iowa as a music major with an emphasis in instrumental music. His instrument of choice was the tuba. Then he fell in love and got married. Having to make a living for his family, he left school to drive an egg truck six days a week, earning $62.80 a week. He and his family lived in a trailer house on his in-laws' land.

Mac tried his hand at cold-call selling and hated it. He tried selling feed and liked that better because the customers came to him, but he was too young and it just didn't work out.

His father was a farmer and his grandfather was a horse puller, and this is where Mac's love of horses came from. His father encouraged him to do something else with his life and said, "Mac, you are tall and you have a good voice; why don't you try to be an auctioneer?"

Mac really wanted to be a music teacher. His whole family loved music. His parents sang and his mother played the piano. Mac played the trumpet when he was in the fifth grade and liked every brass instrument, even the tuba. Today, he plays country guitar and sings country gospel songs. His daughter plays the flute.

Mac went to many auctioneer association seminars and loved the "chant." He explains that the chant is rhythmically saying numbers. Once you get really good at it, like Mac, you can do the chant without thinking about the numbers. It is like singing, and that's why it came naturally to Mac. Mac does a "smooth chant," which is easy to understand even if you are a first-timer at an auction.

Mac took his father's advice and sat in on auctions, really liked them, and learned a lot about them. He liked auctioneering so much that he borrowed four hundred dollars to go to the World Wide College of Auctioneering in Mason City, Iowa.

Shortly after school, while working at a farm store, Mac rented an old building and started having consignment sales of general merchandise, tools, and machinery. He started holding about ten auctions a year. Eventually, Mac left the farm store business and decided to do auctioneering full-time. He had about thirty weekend shows a year, usually off-site. He would have an open house on Friday afternoons for folks to see what he had to auction and then have the actual auction on Saturdays.

Mac did this for ten years. He had a truck and trailers, and he would pack it, ship or haul it, and then sell it. It often takes three days alone to categorize the items and set them up on tables with tablecloths and lighting to really merchandise them correctly. He hired people who knew how to make merchandise look good as well as people who specialized in certain categories like china and crystal.

Mac also worked for Big Bear Farm Stores as a store manager. They sold farm supplies like feed, equipment, parts, and lawn and garden equipment. They also fixed chain saws and other equipment. Mac loved to work on equipment and had a really natural gift for it.

MO!

In the mid '80s, the agricultural business fell on hard times, and Mac decided to go back to auction-eering. He had learned so much about merchandising goods and farm equipment that he knew he could offer full-service to sellers and be a better auctioneer than ever. He has owned more than twenty-five antique John Deere tractors. He restored five of them and sold twenty-one of them before times got tough.

Mac is still an auctioneer to this day. He lives on a twenty-acre farm near Decorah, Iowa, where he raises Belgian horses. He also has some colts and even some mules. He still restores old farm equipment and makes hay to feed his livestock. He belongs to the Horse Plowing Association, holds horse plowing contests, and offers wagon rides in warm weather and sleigh rides in the winter.

Mac has bought and sold so many things in his life, some even over the phone. He recalls bidding $7,750 on a Volkswagen over the phone and does business this way with many out-of-towners. He has kept lots of customers for many years and served families over many generations. He also says that he has sold some of the same things over and over again in the last fifteen years: "They keep coming back because they know I am fair and honest and will get them the best price."

He particularly loves it when he can sell some-thing for more money that the owner asks for. Mac re-calls selling a 1994 Buick that was $10,000 new, and the owner wanted at least $4,000 from the sale. Mac called her after he sold it and said, "I was able to sell your

Buick. Would you take $10,000?" He loves doing this and is often able to get top dollar after he cleans or restores an item. He says, "Often with farm sales, people forget or don't even know what they have in their old barns and on their farms."

Mac gets his leads and much of his business from talking to people everywhere he goes. When you meet Mac, you instantly understand why. Mac has the gift of gab, and it is interesting gab at that! He says if he gets one lead a week, he can turn it into business, and he does! The Saturday after I interviewed him, Mac had an auction with more than $25,000 worth of merchandise his customers turned over to him to sell. And he had a sell out!

Mac has achieved many things in his life. He was honored with the title of Champion Auctioneer in 1980 and was president of the Iowa Auctioneer Board in 1986.

The lessons he has learned are many. He says it best: "It is about long-term relationships. It is about listening and learning from others. It is about surrounding yourself with people who do it better than you. It is realizing that this job is not an eight-hour-a-day job. It may be twelve hours a day for three or four days a week. We all must pay our dues."

Mac has been blessed with a unique talent to fix things that most people would throw out and then sell them with his remarkable gift of "smooth chant" to make a good living and a great life. Mac, you are right, you have seen and sold more than one guy should.

MO! Notes

1. **Build relationships.** Every acquaintance can turn into a long-term relationship and a really good customer at that.

2. **Listen and learn from everyone you meet.** Every other person on Earth knows something you do not. Listen, observe, ask questions, and learn from others. Take a class and find out how to do what you need to do from the experts. Once you learn how, find your own style, and do it as well as you can.

3. **Hang out with people better than yourself.** You cannot be an expert on everything. Find people who specialize in what you do not and let them do what they do best.

4. **Take the time to do the job right.** The amount of time it takes to do a job is not always eight hours a day. Judge a good job by the end result, not by its time frame.

5. **Be honest and fair, always.** People will tell others about you if they feel they have been treated honestly and fairly. This can be the best advertising you could ever have.

6. **Use all your talents.** Like Mac, bundle all your talents into your job. Companies today like one-stop shopping for talent.

7. **There is nothing wrong with hard work.** Somehow, somewhere, we all must pay our dues.

8. **Never give up.** Never feel sorry for yourself, and *never* give up on what you love to do.

meMO!

- Make it a practice to make the very most of meeting each new person in your life. Take time to really listen to what people have to say and ask questions. By asking questions, you learn more than what a person would naturally say themselves. Be more curious every day and then put to practice what you learn from others. Write down the really good lessons on your daily calendar and plan how you will use them.

- Never stop growing and learning. Make it a point to take a class at *least* once a year on a skill that you would like to learn or build. Put it on your calendar and be specific as to when you will start and complete the class. Then make the call or go on the Internet and book it. Halfway through the class, make a list of the next classes you will take and take them.

- Make it a point to have friends of all ages and from all walks of life. We can all learn from each other, regardless of age or vocation. Often what we learn from people of other ages can be translated in some small way to our own lives and possibly to our jobs. If you are hiring people, diversity can enrich your team and your accomplishments.

- Continuing the previous point, surround yourself with people who know more than you about many subjects. Listen to them, and make a journal of what you learn and what you want to use. Each week, implement one lesson until it is part of who you are and how you do things.

- Use all your talents at work. If you know how to change a filter in the copy machine, do it, even if you are the vice president—*really*. Why not? Others will follow, and your team will solidify more each day.

20

Terri Ruff:
A Learner in the World

I remember the first time I met Terri Ruff. She was sitting quietly in the lobby area of a convention center. As I passed her, I smiled and said hello, and she smiled and said hello back. At the time, I was not quite sure why I immediately thought that I had to get to know this lady. Now, after knowing her for a while, I realize what I saw and felt at that first glance was Terri's MO!

Terri is not a big, assuming person with a strong, loud voice. Actually, she is small in stature, with a soft-spoken voice and this sort of hidden half-smile that you know is about to reveal something really wonderful. After you get to know her, you realize she is a great, big, wonderful, loving, learning, teaching "people person." Don't let the small package fool you.

Terri lives in Cincinnati, Ohio, and works for P&G as the human resource manager for the North American division of the Home Care Product Supply Group. Terri says passionately of her job that she feels valued and knows that she makes a difference every single day. Terri is, in her words, "a learner." She loves being in the world, "figuring it out," applying what she has learned, and then teaching it to others. She not only loves learning and teaching, but she also gets to do this every single day.

Terri was born in Cincinnati, grew up in the city, and went to Inner City High School. Her mother stayed at home, raising Terri and her three younger brothers. Her mother was a very wise, behind-the-scenes lady who was the rock and center of the neighborhood. Terri's father was a diversity officer at the post office and a community leader. Terri says of her father, "He was firm, aggressive, and a very proud man. He loved to learn and teach."

Terri started showing her promise early and was valedictorian and president of her senior class. She says this was possible because of strong support from her family as well as a principal and a counselor who both took her under their wings. We all need mentors.

After high school, Terri went to Antioch College and studied finance and accounting. Antioch offered a co-op program where students went to school for six months and then worked for six months to apply what they had learned. Terri actually ended up teaching accounting at the college as a student because they needed a teacher for that class. She loved it, and I am sure she was a natural at it too.

Terri married her high school sweetheart when she was nineteen years old. Less than a month after she graduated college, she gave birth to her first child, a girl.

Terri always knew she wanted to work and learn, learn, learn. Her first real job was for Arthur Anderson as an auditor and public accountant. Terri wanted to get her CPA license, so she took review courses to prepare and did all she could to try to pass the exam. She passed the CPA exam the very first time she took it! This was unprecedented at the time. She needed a minimum grade of 75 to pass, and she got a 75!

Terri is always a very curious person. When you talk with her, she asks lots of questions, and consequently she learns a lot about many things. When she asks her questions you can see she wants to *know*. As a child, she was an avid reader and remembers crying to her mother because she could not figure out a word. She was consistently stubborn about learning and getting all the words right.

Terri says that she is in love with "the sanctuary that is bigger than we are." She explains this to be "working with and teaching the people I interact with, being passionate to serve the love in my soul. It is magic to love yourself, and loving in general is magic!" You don't hear many people say things like that often. It's so refreshing.

Much of this comes from her thirst to learn, and it really picked up steam when she took a course in college on creative intelligence. She learned in this class, by practice and meditation, to control her thoughts and envision what she wanted to occur in her life. Keep in mind, this was before *The Secret* and the current "law of attraction" buzz—this was way before. Terri had the secret long before the book came out! Much of what she envisioned actually did turn into reality for her. It worked! Terri calls it her mental framework. Over the years, she has used this repeatedly to help her achieve what she wanted to accomplish, and it has helped her to be the master of her own fate.

Terri is a realist though. Sometimes people disappoint and make mistakes, and there are times when you just cannot see the good in them. But you do the best with what you have, and the best you have is different from others. *You* are your own unique person! Different is good!

Terri tells a story she calls "Find the Pony." There are two young boys who were brothers; one was an optimist and the other a pessimist. Their parents promised them a pony for Christmas. On Christmas morning, they got up really early and ran to the barn together. The barn was empty except for lots and lots of pony poop. The kid who was the pessimist cried and carried on about there being no pony in the barn, and he was very disappointed. The boy who was the optimist smiled, grabbed a nearby shovel, and started to dig and dig and said, "With all of this poop around, there just has to be a pony in here." Terri says, "As leaders, as teachers of others, you just decide that you are going to find the pony in there." Most of the time you do!

As a young black woman starting in the workforce in the early 1970s, Terri often felt that she was invisible. It was hard to connect on *any* level with the other working people, many of whom were white males. But her faith in who she was and what she had to offer gave her the strength to shine on.

P&G hired Terri thirty-three years ago *while* she was seven months pregnant. She believed in herself, and obviously so did they. She loved herself and never gave up on finding the pony. She found it.

In 1989, Terri divorced her childhood sweetheart, and the same year her dear mother passed away. She says the '90s were a long, dark blur. She had no mother, she had never had any sisters, and she had lost her childhood love. Terri realized that in her family, her mother had done it all. The big, robust family she had was really all because of her mother. Terri realized that she, as the only daughter, had to be the person to carry the torch, pick up the mantel, and keep the family robust. And so she did and still does.

After Terri's mother died, her father eventually remarried. He married the most wonderful woman. They all say that Terri's mother must have sent her to them. Terri's father is now eighty-five years old.

Five years ago, Terri and her family went to a family reunion in Kentucky. They had discovered through researching family history that Terri's father, Alfred Beasley, was really not a Beasley at all. Alfred's mother

(Terri's grandmother) told Alfred when he was growing up that his father was a man named Beasley and that he had died in the 1920s. At that time, she had been living in Kentucky, was pregnant with Alfred, and decided to move to Atlantic City to live with her sister. En route to Atlantic City, there was a very bad snowstorm in Cincinnati, where she got stranded. There, she met a man by the name of Homer Jennings. Terri's grandmother and Homer Jennings fell in love, married, and made a life there. Together they raised Alfred and had more children.

The *true* story Terri's family found out at the reunion was that when Terri's grandmother was living in Kentucky in the 1920s, she got pregnant by a man named Edmond O'Neil. O'Neil was a Harvard-educated schoolteacher who later moved to Connecticut to become a school principal. O'Neil loved children but never had children of his own. To the day he died, he never knew about his son Alfred.

Terry knew a few of her relatives and then met others she did not know about during a family reunion in Kentucky. Terri quickly realized after looking around that a lot of her newly met cousins looked like her and her father! After much storytelling and discussion, the truth about Edmond O'Neil came out. *Wow!* That day, Terri discovered where she and her father got their thirst, hunger, and curiosity for learning, teaching, and getting it right.

Terri's life hasn't been easy. She has worked hard, long hours for many years. She raised her children while working forty hours a week or more. She has ridden a bike to work in order to save up money to buy a car and a home. Always with faith, never wavering, she constantly envisioned what she wanted in her life. Terri says, "The universe cooperates with a made up mind."

Terri has done many jobs during her career at P&G. She has worked in the area of finance as a CPA. She worked for thirteen years in Lexington, Kentucky, with a P&G company bottler doing what an engineer would do. She also ran a warehouse for the Jiff peanut butter brand. Terri told me about how she would talk to, teach, and encourage the hourly folks while running the warehouse. She would always tell them to just do their best. She gave them the respect they deserved. She says, "I learned a lot from those folks. They and that experience have made me who I am today. What I learned from those hourly people is forever; it goes up above and beyond the job, it changed my life and how I do my job today."

Terri's mantra is simple: There is magic in each individual. Show them you see it, treat them as they are worthy, tell them they have potential, teach them what you know, give them the attention they need, and coach them with love. Show them the possibilities.

Terri is happily married and has a daughter, a son, a stepson, and two granddaughters. She continues to inspire and make a difference with all the people she meets along the way. She knows she will continue to do this; she sees it on the road ahead because she has made up her mind to do so.

MO! Notes

1. **Think.** Practice focusing on what you want in your life instead of what you don't want. What you think about you can bring about.

2. **Celebrate.** Rejoice in the miracles and surprises in life, especially with family.

3. **Be part of your family tree.** You have a family. Carry the family torch when it is your turn.

4. **Have respect.** Always treat others, both above you and below you, with dignity and respect. They may just change your life for the better.

5. **Learn.** Be ferocious and constant about learning.

6. **Teach.** Remember to teach others what you know. The gift will be yours.

7. **Have style.** A quiet but confident voice can be heard loud and clear.

8. **Focus on your goals.** Focus on what you know of yourself and your own capabilities. Never give up on believing in yourself.

meMO!

- When something great happens, make a point to celebrate it for an entire day—*really!* Schedule the celebration on your calendar and celebrate the event.

- Be ferocious and persistent about learning. Make a list of three things you want to learn or be better at. Be specific as to when you want to have accomplished each goal. Go to the Internet or the Yellow Pages, find someone who offers the education you want, pick up the phone, and sign up for the first available opportunity. Complete it and move on to the next one on your list.

- When talking to others, do it in a teaching style with a soft voice. If you tell instead of sell or lecture, it will be much more effective.

- Never sell yourself short. Make a list of your strengths and capabilities. Focus on these in your daily job. Read this list first thing each morning and last thing at night. As you grow and change, modify your list and keep going.

21

Willie Morris:
Always a Pleasure
to Talk to You

On any given weekday, you can depend on seeing Mr. Willie Morris at his shoeshine stand at the airport in Fort Lauderdale, Florida. If he is not busy shining a customer's shoes at his stand, you can count on him to be walking around saying hello to travelers on their way to their boarding gates or having a warm conversation with an old-time frequent flying customer.

Willie Morris has worked for Pernell's Super Shoe Shine Company for nineteen years. When I called the main office of Pernell's to get Willie's direct phone number, the owner, Ms. Jessie Pernell, said to me, "Oh yes, Mr. Morris does have a cell phone, and I will get you the number." From that day forward, Willie has been Mr. Morris to me.

I have known Mr. Morris almost since the first day he worked at the airport. At first, I would pass his stand on the way to my boarding gate and he would always say hello. We became casual "Hello, how are you today" friends. He would always end each of our short conversations with, "Always a pleasure to talk to you."

Mr. Morris had never shined my shoes. You see, I always felt funny about having my shoes shined, being a girl and all. Wasn't this only for men? Hopping up on his high stool and having my girl shoes shined was just a bit strange to me.

Then one day on the way to my boarding gate as I was passing the Super Shoe Shine stand, Mr. Morris said hello and looked down at my feet and said, "Let me shine those pretty boots you have on there." I hopped up on his stool and the rest is history. He polished my boots to the shine of "new," and as I hopped down from his stool, he said, "Always a pleasure to talk to you." I was hooked. He is really good at shoe shining and gets any shoes looking like new, and he does it quickly too. Mr. Morris told me that he has to be fast, because his customers have places to go and can't miss their planes.

While your shoes are being shined, he talks about what he is doing to keep your shoes looking great, what he is using, and why he is using it on your shoes. I learned from him that shining shoes is like painting a wall that has wallpaper on it; you have to remove the old polish before you put on the new polish and re-member to shine and seal them, too. Mr. Morris says, "This is really important if your shoes are exposed to the cold and if they get wet." I learned a lot about why I need to take care of my shoes and why Mr. Morris is the one to do it. I also learned one of the reasons Mr. Morris keeps on talking to his customers: "If I don't talk to them, they won't talk to me." Most people just watch as their shoes are being shined, read the paper, or just sit there doing nothing. Mr. Morris makes it enter-taining, fun, and educational all while he is giving you the best darn shoeshine you will ever have—*ever!* No wonder everyone keeps coming back.

Mr. Morris still takes care of my shoes, my hus-band's shoes, and most of the shoes of the business travelers that are frequent flyers through the Fort Lau-derdale airport.

Before 9/11 when nontraveling passengers could go beyond security to the boarding gate area where Pernell's Super Shoe Shine stand is, many locals would bring bags of shoes to Mr. Morris to shine and then pick them up on another day. Mr. Morris had lockers at his shoeshine stand where he could securely store his customers' shoes for them. In those days, there were hardly any places to get a really good shoeshine other than airports, and if you think about it, this is truer than ever today.

Mr. Morris tells me that a lot of the younger guys these days just wear their shoes unpolished and torn up. Come on guys, get with the program! Many of his "big, regular frequent flyers" will sit to have the shoes they have on shined and also a pair or two that are in their carry-ons. Smart!

I asked Mr. Morris if the fashion of people wearing sneakers has affected his shoeshine business, and he said, "No, my main customers are business travelers who wear leather shoes or boots, and some wear synthetic rubber or plastic, and they need to be conditioned too." Who knew?

It is obvious that Mr. Morris loves what he does. He says, "My customers depend on me being here when they come through. So I am." He works twelve hours a day, five days a week, every week.

Before he was a super shoeshiner, he built pools for a while and then worked for himself landscaping and hauling trash. He says, "I did the really hard work first."

Mr. Morris is a rare native Floridian. He was born in 1958 and raised in Fort Lauderdale. He is the youngest child of five: three boys and two girls. His mother lives in Tampa, and his dad passed away in 1997. Mr. Morris has been married for thirty-four years and has four children: two daughters and two sons. His children say that he is really good at being their father too.

I can never pass Mr. Morris's stand without him giving me a great, big, warm greeting, asking about how my family is and then talking about the boots that he first shined for me nineteen years ago.

Mr. Morris says hello to everyone that passes by Pernell's Super Shoe Shine stand in the Fort Lauderdale airport. He is a true professional, and even if he has shined your shoes just one time, he will remember your shoes, he will probably remember exactly what kind they were, and most of all he will always remember *you*.

Mr. Morris makes you feel like his very best customer, *always*. Thank you, Mr. Morris.

MO! Notes

1. **Make everyone feel like your best customer.** They will reward you with their ongoing business.

2. **Remember people's faces.** Who doesn't like to be remembered?

3. **Don't be silent when selling.** Keep talking and telling your customer what they need to know about what you are doing. Teach and they will remember.

4. **Look.** If you are taking care of someone's hair, you look at their haircut, and if you are taking care of someone's stocks, you look at their stock portfolio. So if you are taking care of someone's shoes, remember to look at their feet.

5. **Find your niche.** Offer a service or product that is needed by consumers and hard to find and be the best at it.

6. **Out with the old.** Remember to have the old shoe polish removed before you put on the new, and always seal, too.

7. **Start strong and finish strong.** Have a great, smiling "hello" and an even better "good-bye." (Like Mr. Morris says, "It is always a pleasure to talk to you."). This can become your signature, and people will remember you for it.

meMO!

- Practice your smiling "hello" and your signature "good-bye" everywhere you go and with everyone you meet. After you start doing this for a few days, it will become a habit. It will make others feel great, and it will make *you* feel good too.

- Practice being observant. Every working hour, make a point to observe something about another and comment on it. For example, "I like your new haircut," "Your fragrance is really pretty," and so on. People like to be noticed, and it can enrich a relationship or strike up conversations with people you might not necessarily talk with otherwise.

22

Goldie Brown: Slipcover Maven

Perhaps "Goldie Lee Brown" got her name because of the color of her hair. She certainly looked like a Goldie: her hair was a lovely, golden tone; her skin was peaches and cream; and she had the youngest, clearest speaking voice you could imagine.

Goldie Brown was born in Elk Fork, Kentucky, and moved to Logan, West Virginia, in high school. She started sewing at the age of fourteen and was self-taught.

Goldie married young and had a son shortly after. One day, the baby spit up on her couch, and the spot would not come out. Being young and not having a lot of money, she could not afford to have the couch recovered. Goldie decided to try to make a slipcover for it, and that was where it all started.

Her mother-in-law thought she did a "really good job" with the slipcover and asked if she would make one for her. Goldie did. Soon after, others were asking Goldie to make slipcovers for them, and she did.

Word got out around the town, and before Goldie knew it, a business was born. She was working almost every day, making slipcovers for friends, neighbors, relatives, and eventually strangers. A local store called Stone and Thomas heard about her and recommended her to customers who bought fabric from them.

She eventually moved to Louisville, Kentucky, with her family where she once again made a very successful business, pleasing clients and covering furniture every day. She also made covers for pillows and anything else that needed to be covered. She was an expert zipper lady, too.

Goldie's work was fairly priced, precise, professionally done, and so good it was often hard to tell that what was covering the couch was a slipcover at all; you might have thought it was upholstered. She *was* good!

Goldie collected and used three sewing machines, all Singers. One of them was about sixty years old. That one was her favorite. "It still works just fine," she told me.

Once, a client who had work for Goldie called her to ask when she was able to start the project. Goldie said, "It will be a few more days. I am still at Sue's house, and the work is a little more than I thought here.

I think I have covered everything in the house except for the cat!"

The beauty of what Goldie did is that she went to the client's home with her sewing machine and the tools of her trade in tow and did the work right there, so furniture did not have to be hauled around. Goldie liked it that way because she also didn't have the cleanup at home, she had low overhead, and sometimes she even got lunch. *Smart!*

Goldie did not use scissors or measuring tape when cutting and sizing fabric to fit. Yes, that's right; she just used her hands. When you saw her do this, it could be a little unnerving, especially if you had spent one hundred dollars a yard for fabric. You might think, *What the heck is she doing? Does she really know what she is doing?* You see, what she did was take the bolt of fabric and unroll it, and with her arms spread wide, she visually measured one, two, three feet of fabric up against the couch or chair to fit it for sizing. Once she had determined how much she was going to use for the piece, she took the end of the fabric and ripped it with her hands. *It worked!* Goldie said, "Ripping the fabric is a lot faster, and you also get a much straighter line then cutting." Who knew? Goldie did.

She then went to work on her sewing machine, often set up on a card table or dining table right in the room where the furniture was to be covered, zipping along at record speed with the precision and vision of an artist. It was clear that Goldie loved what she did. You could see it in the quality of her work, in her unending energy, and in her passion for what she was doing.

After her husband passed away in Louisville, Goldie moved to Fort Lauderdale, Florida, where she lived and worked with her very successful business for many years. Then Goldie moved back to Louisville to be closer to her sister and family. Shortly after settling in, she once again established her business and did very well. Many of her clients from Florida kept calling her, asking when she could come to visit and do some work for them. A few clients even got together and paid for a ticket to fly her back to Florida. Goldie loved this, and of course she did the work.

She once had a Florida client call to request another slipcover for his couch. The old one she had made needed to be replaced. He asked if he could send her the old slipcover so she could make another one just like it. She said, "I am afraid not, it would be better and faster if you sent the couch!" Goldie explained that it was more difficult and time-consuming to disassemble a slipcover and make a pattern than it was just to start from scratch. Who knew? Goldie did.

Goldie just loved what she did for lots of reasons. She said, "It gives me a good living, and I get to go to a different place almost every day, see different homes, each with a different décor, and I get to meet nice people along the way too." Her philosophy was, "The more you go and do, the more you get to do."

Goldie was still going and doing and getting to go and do more every day. The day before we talked to her about her life, she told us she sold her car and her clients picked her up and took her to their homes. It worked nicely for Goldie; you see, Goldie was born on

December 13, 1913. She was ninety-six years young and still going strong. She had outlived her husband, her son, her sister, and many of her friends, but her verve and vigor for life remained a wonderful gift to all that knew and loved her. She had covered a lot of furniture, traveled a lot of miles, and certainly changed our lives for the better just by being herself. Yes, Goldie did.

Goldie Brown passed away on November 11, 2009. She will be missed by all who had the pleasure of knowing her lovely sprit.

MO! Notes

1. **Keep moving.** The more you do, the more you get to do. An object in motion tends to stay in motion. If you keep up your energy and momentum, *things happen!*

2. **Know what you are good at.** Like Goldie, find what you like to do and are good at and try it. Once you find some success, build on that and stay the course.

3. **Find your niche.** Once you find out what you're good at, find a way to really focus on it. Niche businesses are always needed. Try to find a niche that few others fill.

4. **Try to do it faster and perhaps easier.** Like Goldie ripping fabric instead of cutting it, try to find a way to do what you are doing more efficiently. This can save time and usually money. Time often means money.

5. **Produce with quality.** Regardless of what you do or make, do it with the very best quality you can. People will recommend you, remember you, and call you again and again.

meMO!

- If you are looking for a new business opportunity niche businesses often work. Offering a service or product that is needed by consumers, and perhaps hard to find are best. Look around your community and make a list of the types of businesses that are in cluster retail areas. Decide what business you might be able to perform well in. Look around your community at another cluster retail area that might need that particular business and go from there. For example, there might be a successful car wash on the east side of town but none on the west side of town.

- Start remembering people's names. It is an easy thing to do if you use the association technique. For example, if you meet a person named Mrs. Appletree and she has a round face like an apple and she is tall, these two things will help you remember her name. Try it daily. The more you do this, the better you will get at it. People like to be remembered.

23

Beatriz Farland:
Be Inspired, Be Giving,
Be Positive

Beatriz Farland, or "B" as she prefers to be called, was born in Chicago and moved to South Florida at the age of four. She grew up there, raised a family, and has a fitness studio that changes people lives for the better. You might say she is MOtivated to help people get healthy.

Let's face it, most of us don't leap at the chance to take a spinning or Pilates class first thing in the morning, but B's students do. What's her secret? She believes in herself, and through this she inspires others to be the best they can be.

B loves to dance and was on her high school dance team. She also played tennis. After she graduated from high school, she started at Broward Community College (BCC). B joined a gym at the age of seventeen and started teaching step aerobics classes the same year.

When B took her first step class, she *loved* it. It was physical and rhythmic like dance and so natural to her. The step instructor thought B was so good she put her in a contest with sixty other girls from the fitness center. Although B really did not want to enter the contest, she was persuaded, and she ended up winning. From there she gained a sense of confidence.

One day, a step instructor did not show up for a class, and the owner of the center asked B if she would teach it. B said, "Oh no, I'm too shy." The owner said, "You have to." B considered it and thought, "What a great opportunity to get over my fears and do something I love and be able to share that love with others." She agreed to teach the step class. Reflecting back on that day, B says she was awful and she was scared, but she remembers saying to herself, *I can do this*. So she did.

When B is scared or shy, has a big challenge, or thinks she cannot do something, she has always had something deep inside of her that tells her, *Try it. You can do this and you will succeed*. This is an inner driving voice that B uses to challenge herself and her clients. "We all have so much more potential in us; we just have to take ourselves out of our comfort zones and have a positive outlook to find that out."

B loved the experience of teaching her first fitness class so much that she got certified while going to college. After two years at BCC, B went to Florida State University (FSU), where she tried out to become one of the university's group exercise instructors. This was the first time she had to audition to be an instructor, and she was up against a very large and tough group of instructors who all wanted this amazing opportunity as well. When she got the position, she was so happy and excited. She taught classes to more than sixty students at a time and says it was one of the best experiences she has ever had in her career. She gained tremendous confidence during her teaching years at FSU.

After college, B worked at several fitness studios with the dream that someday she would have her own. She wanted to create a place "that is not competitive, where people think and feel like I do." B thought to herself, "I can do this!" Her goal was to give each client a feeling of positive energy and positive support. She wanted to create a place that focused on balanced life: a space where there was great personal attention, where people felt good and safe, and where everyone knew your name—a fitness studio that inspired confidence.

In January 2010, B did just that, and Studio BE opened. The name came to her one day as she was out running alone; she thought about what the studio would be about. Then it came to her: "Be strong, Be inspiring, Be happy, Be balanced, Be giving"—basically, just "Be." Studio BE has a menu of classes: Spinning, Pilates, Boot Camp, Xtend Ballet Barre, and more. B says that the Xtend Ballet Barre class is like "Pilates amped up." With this class, B feels like she has come full circle back to her first fitness love: dance.

B inspires her students to try, to feel like they can do it, and to find the voice inside of them that says, *Let out all the stuff inside that is holding you back from doing this: you can do this*. "Stay away from any negative voices or people that hold you back," B says. "This is your life, and we all deserve to be as happy and healthy as we can be."

B's clients are like family to her; she says they inspire her more than she inspires them. They inspired her to do her first marathon, her first 150-mile bike ride, and her first half Ironman and to open her own studio, because they knew she could do it. She is grateful to all the people that have come and gone and that continue to be in her life that helped her along her journey.

In April 2010, B gave birth to her first child, Sebastian, who is the love of her life. She found out she was pregnant the same week she decided to open Studio BE. She feels there was a higher reason these two things happened at the same time.

Throughout her entire pregnancy, B continued to be active and gave classes until two weeks before her son was born. It was a great and healthy pregnancy. B says of exercise, "This stuff really works," and she started walking after the baby was born. Even after having a nine-pound baby and a C-section, she still recovered very quickly. She was back to work and back to working out stronger than ever.

The experience of having a baby and all the things the body goes through during and after has enabled B to help other women going through it. She now knows what it takes to get in shape and all that it takes to stay there.

B has seen so many fitness folks doing too much, overdoing workouts, and injuring themselves. People often overdo fitness because it allows them to emotionally run away from something, and the fitness high makes them feel good for a while. Through her years of experience, she has learned that exercise is key to being happy but that overdoing anything is never good. She makes it her goal to teach balance and safety while exercising.

B teaches that exercise = happiness = balance. Life to B is about balance, health, family, and career in that order.

B often talks as she teaches her spinning classes, and it is often self-talk that she shares with her students. She relates the spinning ride to life. She says things like, "If you think about negatives, stop it, and remember, 'I believe in myself; I like *me*.' Don't let people rent space in your head; stay away from negative energy. Create positive energy and share it with others. Give it away! Believe in yourself. Life has hills just like this spin class, and how you take it on shows your strength to get through anything tough. Sometimes it's good to get out of your comfort zone and see what you're really made of." She also takes people to their feel-good zone throughout the ride, asking students to think of something that makes them smile and to really focus on it. Her motive going into each class is to give her students 100 percent of herself, and her goal is that they walk away from the class more positive than when they arrived. She explains that sometimes there is a little hurt, but with a few more pushes and a little more endurance, you can make it through anything and come out stronger, just like in *life*.

B uses fitness analogies in most things that she does. She likened her pregnancy to doing a half Ironman competition. The first trimester was a 1.2-mile swim in open waters: not too hard, but uncomfortable with some nervous, anxious feelings. The second trimester was a 56-mile bike ride: most of the time she was on cloud nine, feeling confident and great (this is her favorite activity). The third trimester was a half-marathon run. She says she was saying to herself, "This is getting hard, but I am almost there, and I can feel the sense of victory and accomplishment, and I can see the finish line."

B has now been teaching for more than twenty years and still gets just as excited before each class as she did when she was seventeen.

MO! Notes

1. **Face your demons head-on daily.** We all have fears or insecurities. Know what they are, and face them with a can-do attitude and a positive outlook. It has been said by successful people that if one person can do it, so can others!

2. **Use your strengths to their fullest and see how you can inspire others.** When people see true strength in others, it is quite natural

for them to be inspired. It is human nature to love to see someone *try*.

3. **Follow your dreams.** If you love something that you do, do it to the best of your ability. Throw yourself into it fully and take it as far as you can. It may bring you great success, and if it doesn't, something else will show up for you, and you can try that.

4. **Take lessons from the people in your life— even the little people.** Stay in tune with how others affect you emotionally, mentally, and physically. Observe, learn, and pass it on. B did just this. Fitness really helped her get back into shape after her baby was born, and being surrounded by positive energy at her studio made all the difference in the world.

5. **Self-talk really works.** Just like we really are what we eat, we really are and can become what we tell ourselves we are. What you think about, you bring about.

meMO!

- Decide what your biggest strength is, use it, and focus your actions on it every single day and in all you do.

- Focus your career path on a job that utilizes your strengths. Write them down on paper for clarity, and look at your list daily.

- If you have always had a dream to do something in your life, make a short-term and long-term plan on paper to map out how you can get there. Every day and in everything you do, work toward this goal.

- Think about one thing you are afraid of, and work on facing it head-on every day. You will eventually become comfortable with it and learn to overcome this fear. Then move on to another fear you have and do the same.

- When you see others who inspire you even in a small way, think about how you can apply what you learned from this inspiration to your daily life and *do* it.

CHAPTER

24

MO! Thoughts

We feel very fortunate to have had the experience of interviewing all the amazing people who are featured in this book. We have learned so much and been so inspired by their examples. As we interviewed people, we had many questions we continued to ask ourselves, and we were consumed with curiosity as to *what makes a successful person tick*. As we let others know we were writing the book, they had questions as well. Here are some of the questions that have been rattling around in our minds throughout this entire process.

Are People Born with MO! or Do They Just Develop It Along the Way?

That is a fascinating, age-old question. Is it nature or nurture? We believe that there are people who certainly are born with some personal characteristics that make them more *likely* to have MOtivation, MOmentum, and MOxie. However, we also noted in many of our interviews that even if you were born with those qualities, life (who seems to be a stand-up comedian) often has a funny way of testing your level of MO! Many of our subjects were faced with tremendous amounts of soul-crushing adversity, but despite that adversity—yes, you guessed it—they remained MOtivated.

Are People Who Have MO! in Any Particular Demographic Group?

The answer is without a doubt *no*. No. No. No. No. OK, enough no's. The people we interviewed who have these special qualities are not restricted to a particular label of gender, race, creed, color, ethnicity, or religion. In fact, it almost seems to be the opposite. People with these special qualities seem to transcend the label that the world at large wishes to apply to them. It's almost as if it does not matter to them. They refuse to be labeled and do not allow any label to hold them back. We saw people with MO! who were only sixteen years old and people with MO! who were super senior citizens. Age seemed not to matter to them; in most cases, they chose to ignore it. Age is only a number! This is where the mental aspect comes into play.

Do People Who Have MO! Know That They Have It?

That is also an interesting question. We found that many of the people we interviewed possessed a humble attitude and were very interested in serving others.

They were confident but not arrogant, not bashful but also not boastful. If you asked each one of them if they were motivated, our guess is they would probably reply, "I'm not sure if I am motivated, but I am an optimistic person." What we do know is that other people who meet those with MO! can automatically tell they have it. They have a spark, energy, enthusiasm, and passion for life and for people, and as we described in many cases, they are like magnets that draw other people to them. It's kind of like the definition of great art: it's hard to describe, but you know it when you see it. The special people contained within the pages of this book are people magnets. They inspire and motivate others.

Can Someone Learn to Develop His or Her Level of MO!?

Of course! If we did not believe that people could develop this skill set, then there would be no point in writing this book. The entire point of this book is to acknowledge that people do have the power and the ability to change their mind-set and change their life. We encourage you to go back to each chapter and reread the MO! Notes and meMOs at the end to figure out how you can apply them to your life. We believe that what you have, what you do, and how you feel about it is entirely up to you. You are the architect of your own life, so build it. Humans are the only species that we know of who have the ability to change their lives through the act of conscious thought. We have never seen a turtle sitting on a log with a planner in his hand. Everyone that we interviewed reinforced these exact concepts over and over.

Why Does Having MO! Matter?

Well, it is actually quite simple. People are attracted to people who have MOtivation, MOmentum, and MOxie. If you do not believe this to be true, here are a few questions to ask yourself: If you were an employer, would you want to hire an employee who had these qualities or one who did not? If you were dating, would you want to date someone who had these qualities or someone who did not? If you were trying to find someone to be your best friend, would you want somebody who had these qualities or somebody who did not? How about choosing someone to talk to at a party? How about choosing your doctor or dentist, or the passenger in the seat next to you on the plane ride to Buffalo, or your cube mate at work? Invariably, the answers to all these questions would be a person with MO! Since this is true, then *you* want to be someone who has MO!, and you want to be with people who have MO!

Isn't the Concept of Everyone Having MO! Unrealistic?

Yes. No. Maybe. Whatever the answer, these two authors will continue to be unrealistic, overoptimistic dreamers. We plead guilty and throw ourselves at the mercy of the world court! The reality is that we don't care about the verdict. Being folks with MO! ourselves, we believe that everybody has the capability to live up to his or her full potential. We also believe that everyone can develop increased levels of MOtivation, MOmentum, and MOxie. Will everyone have MO!? No, because some people will reject the concept entirely and will continue to be cynical, negative naysayers. That is their choice; it is their freedom. People can decide to be unMOtivated, have no MOmentum, and have no MOxie. They also have the choice to be miserable and depressed. That *is* a choice. One of the key elements we found in the people we interviewed was that every one of them just flat-out *decided* to reinvent their lives, to be motivated, and to refuse to listen to the cynical, negative people in the world. So if everyone having MO! is unrealistic, that is OK with us. We still choose it. We take what is behind door #3. There will always be some people who are too shortsighted or stubborn to change and are satisfied with living life with limitations. Too sad—it will be their limited life.

In our interviews, we were delighted with the variety of people, personalities, and occupations we got to know. We also wondered if there was some sort of commonality among the entire group that we could point to and say, "Here is what these folks have in common." Was there a thread?

We have been able to identify fifteen traits that all these folks seem to have in common:

1. **They want to be the best.** Everyone we talked to has an overwhelming desire and an internal drive to be the best at what they do and the best person that they can be. It doesn't matter whether they run a fitness studio, check in baggage, or are professional speakers; they have a commitment to being the best and take real pride in their work. They don't always need a reason. You could assume that they developed that attitude from the people who

raised them, but as you have already read, there are many exceptions to prove that this is not true. Many folks we interviewed had developed the attitude on their own, despite the fact that they were in abusive or negative situations. You might describe them as self-made, which gives hope to all of us.

2. **They have a positive attitude.** No matter what happens, they look at life through a lens that is colored for happiness. The glass is half full. They truly look on the bright side of life. Many folks that we spoke to surprised us by saying that they decide to be happy no matter what happens to them. It is a stubborn form of happiness. Every day when these folks get up, they decide to be happy. Even though they may be in jobs in which they're required to serve hot dogs, process fish, or handle luggage, they still get up every day with a positive attitude, actually looking forward to their work rather than dreading it. In fact, their glass is always *more* than half full. They don't understand people who see the glass as half empty. They can make lemonade out of pickle juice!

3. **They have faced adversity.** The people we interviewed have faced every range of adversity from racism to physical and mental abuse to being poor to nearly dying of circumstances that were either in or out of their control. The key with every one of these people is that no matter what the adversity was, they got right

back up again and just kept going. They're like the old-fashioned inflatable punch toy that is weighted on the bottom. You punch it and it just swings back up. Many of them remind us of the song by the band Chumbawamba called "Tubthumping," where in the chorus they gleefully sing, "I get knocked down, but I get up again! You're never going to keep me down!" These folks don't believe in giving up. It's not an option! Adversity will not win in their lives.

4. **They embrace opportunity.** Every single person that we talked to embraces opportunity when it comes to him or her, whether it is difficult or not. They have the uncanny ability to identify a short-term opportunity that will lead to long-term success. They trust their guts. They also embrace opportunity even when they face fearful situations or situations in which they have to learn new skills. To them, it really doesn't matter if it is new — they just keep plowing forward, knowing that things will work out. Many of them also state that they are willing to change their occupation multiple times and will try one type of work, then another, and another until they find the right fit for their talents. How many people say, "I'm afraid to leave the job I have because I might not like the next one"? These fine people don't. Their philosophy is, "If I have an opportunity, I'm going to take advantage of it."

5. **They love hard work.** Every person we interviewed has the amazing work ethic of a Morgan plow horse. They work hard, have worked hard, and continue to work hard. They know the value of hard work and really don't mind doing it. Their work may be hard physically or mentally or they may have more than one job at the same time, but they never complain about it or even make it sound like a negative. They just do what they do, and they keep doing it. They love it. Additionally, many of these people not only are working hard but also are busy with other life activities while they are working. Laziness is a foreign concept to people with MO!, and they don't understand it. Lazy is just not in their DNA. They think it is crazy to be lazy.

6. **They are persistent.** Every person in this book has enduring, dogged persistence. They might have to ride a bicycle thirty-one miles, put up with abuse, work long hours with low pay, or work for managers they don't agree with, but they are always persistent and always have an idea of what they are going to do in the future. Many times they would say things like "I don't give up," or "I don't quit," or "There is no quit in me." They simply don't view quitting as a viable option. This is a very admirable quality and one that many people in the world don't have. People often give up right before they have reached a level of success. The quality of MO! means that one doesn't ever give up.

7. **They tap into resources.** People with MO! don't leave things to chance; they look around to find resources that are available to them. It might be a book, a church, a mentor, or a training program, but these people do not sit around on their hands waiting for something—not a chance. They find a resource and tap into it. We also found that they are willing to ask other people where the resources are located and how to find them. They realize that someone out there knows what they need to know and that someone has been successful at it before them. They are not necessarily wise; they seek wisdom from those who possess it. They know where to find it or, if they don't, they just keep looking. They ask, question, investigate, research, and keep at it.

8. **They don't limit their thinking.** They are not tied to a limited belief system that says that they can't do what they want to do. Their position, background, and economic status are irrelevant. Why can't they be millionaires? Why can't they start businesses from scratch and have them be successful? Why can't they change the world around them and have an impact? Why can't they move to a foreign country? Why can't they start a revolution? They are not defined by a label. People telling them that they can't does not discourage them. It does the opposite, in fact: it motivates them to prove to those people that their negative thinking is flawed.

They refuse to think in a small way; they only think about the massive possibilities and know that it starts with their thinking first. These people are big thinkers. They set goals some others would think are crazy and unrealistic, but they are really not too concerned with the opinions of skeptics.

9. **They are learners.** All the people we interviewed are not just learners; many of them are what we call "superlearners." They have an innate sense of curiosity about how things work. They have gone to school, gone to training programs, gone to colleges, gotten certifications, and read tons of books. They all understand that in order to be successful they need to keep learning and keep growing. They do not believe in stagnation, only motivation. They are always trying to figure out what they can learn and where they can learn it. Learning, for them, is a lifelong process. They want the MOhow, and they want it now.

10. **They are unique.** People with MO! don't seem to be very interested in fitting in with the crowd or being like everyone else. They are proud to be unique and don't mind other people thinking of them as eccentric. The pressures of society do not sway them; they are more interested in doing what it takes to accomplish their goals. Ironically, the fact that they are not so interested in conforming to social norms makes them admired by those who don't have the courage to be

different. The very society that gives them a hard time for being different one day admires them the next.

11. **They embrace life.** Everyone that we interviewed took life by the horns and wrestled it to the ground. They embrace life with a spirit of vim and vigor. They realize that life is short, and they make sure they treat every day with the value it deserves. They are people who accomplish things, get things done, and are the "doers" of our world. At the same time, they also enjoy life overall, embracing their experiences and their passions. They are the kind of people who do not want to retire at the end of their life and look back consumed by the disease of regret. They will make mistakes, but no one will ever accuse them of not embracing life to the fullest.

12. **They are brave.** They have courage, determination, and a spirit of getting it done. This "give it a try" attitude allows them to attempt things that other people would often not even consider doing. They face their demons. After all, starting your own business is risky and fraught with difficulties, and it leads to some anxious moments. The folks we interviewed, however, have always felt that the risks will always be outweighed by the rewards in the end. If you're not willing to take the risks, then you will not be able to gain the rewards. These people are willing to take a shot.

13. **They have heroes and mentors.** Many of the people we interviewed mentioned a hero or mentor that they had learned a great deal from. It may have been a parent, a teacher, a business partner, a friend, or even a person in a book, but they found someone in their lives that could help them, guide them, direct them, or support them. These mentors and heroes obviously had a tremendous impact, and our subjects were always willing to give them full credit for their assistance. We suspect that most successful people in life have been shaped by mentors and heroes, and those who are not as successful have not sought out such mentors and heroes in their lives.

14. **Be willing to give up the hunt.** Everyone in life has failures in either their personal or their professional lives. (Probably both.) The folks we talked to were very persistent, but they also had the common sense to know when it was time to give something up and move on to some other endeavor. Let's face it: sometimes the rocket does not leave the pad, sometimes you fail a test, or sometimes you lose a friend. Sometimes the homecoming queen goes out with someone else. (Darn.) These people were willing to face their failures and simply move on to something else without letting these missteps define their future in a negative way.

15. **They follow their instincts.** Many times when we asked people why they did something or

took some sort of action, they said they just had a gut instinct or felt it was the right thing to do. They would even say, "I don't know... I just had a feeling." The difference between these people and people who do not have MO! is that they are willing to listen to their instincts, trust their gut, and take action accordingly, because they trust themselves.

Are the subjects featured in our book all perfect? Of course not; they are human beings with quirks and frailties like anyone else. We are all flawed in this life. However, these folks do possess very special qualities that we can all learn from if we are willing to open our eyes, our ears, and our hearts.

They volunteered to share their stories in the hope that they would help you improve your life. We felt a particularly vital responsibility to do justice to each of these special, wonderful people. Telling someone else's story is always something we feel a little more serious about; we are writing about *his or her* truth.

As we close out this first book of MO!, we thank you for spending time with us, and we beg you to embrace this content and apply it to *your* world. (Yes, there will be more books in the future! To quote the Carpenters, "We've only just begun.")

Here is what we have learned that we would like to leave you with in closing.

If in reading this you have determined that you are unhappy with all or part of your life, then change it. You have the ability to change, as you are, after all, the architect of your own existence. We have both seen in our careers as speakers and trainers tremendous success stories: people who changed because they decided to. It is our heartfelt hope that we have had an impact on your life by sharing these stories. There is always someone else in life that we can learn from. There will always be someone who knows something we do not. You can continue to learn. You can continue to reinvent yourself.

We want you to realize from reading these stories that anything is possible. We believe many of the people in this book will achieve the next levels of their big dreams. Anything truly *is* possible, and history has certainly taught us that. Remember that people were sent to the moon only as the result of a group of human beings who thought it was possible. Many people said it was a ridiculous, fruitless effort and it would never happen. History proved them wrong.

So here is the big question: Are you going to allow your past to determine your future or the cynical people of the world to define your path? We hope not. We hope that this book and these amazing stories of people with MO! will help convince you that you can live an amazing life of personal and professional excellence with rewards beyond your wildest dreams.

We hope you enjoyed this book. *Now go out and find YOUR MO!*

About Shawn Doyle

Shawn Doyle is a learning and development professional and a certified speaking professional who has a passion for human potential. He has an avid belief in the concept of lifelong learning. For the last twenty years, Shawn has spent his time developing and implementing training programs on team-building, communication, creativity, and leadership. This has been to help people become more effective in the workplace and in their lives. Some clients include Pfizer, Comcast, Charter Media, IBM, Kraft, Microsoft, the Marine Corps, TheLadders.com, and Los Alamos National Defense Laboratory.

He is available to provide the following services:

- Speaking at your next meeting

- Sales, motivational, or leadership training

- Custom training

- Executive coaching

- Life coaching

- Sales coaching

If you would like to contact Shawn with questions or comments, send him an e mail at SLDoyle1@aol.com. Visit his website for free articles and other resources: http://www.sldoyle.com.

About Lauren Anderson

With her continual reinvention of programs, cutting edge ideas, motivational style, and savvy media skills, Lauren Anderson is highly sought after as a consultant, mentor, and spokesperson. She is a frequent and recognizable guest on national television and writes many articles for top specialty and professional publications. Lauren belongs to numerous business associations all over the country and participates in many charitable and fundraising events. She is also cofounder of the East Side Clickers, a business networking group in South Florida. Anderson is working on two books based on her wide-ranging experiences. She lives in Fort Lauderdale, Florida, with her family.

To find out more about Lauren, visit http://www.laurenanderson.com.

MO! Notes

MO! Notes

MO! Notes

MO! Notes

MO! Notes

MO! Notes

MO! Notes